SPACE-TIME TALK

New Testament Hermeneutics
A Philosophical and Theological
Approach

by

Mark Chungmoon Chang

With a Foreword by Professor John
Macquarrie

Heritage Research House, Inc.
1988

SPACE-TIME TALK: New Testament Hermeneutics--A Philosophical and Theological Approach by Mark Chungmoon Chang

Library of Congress Cataloging in Publication Data

Chang, Mark Chungmoon, 1930-
    Space-time talk.

    (HRH publication ; no.2)
    Revision of the author's thesis (Ph. D.)--Pacific Western University, Los Angeles.
    Bibliography: p.
    Includes Index.
    1. Bible. N.T.--Hermeneutics. 2. Space and time--Biblical teaching. I. Title. II. Series.
    BS2331.C45   1988   225.6'01   88-28422
    ISBN 0-912617-02-0

Printed in the United States of America

To

My Parents,
My Wife,
and
Bishop Paul C. Lee

About the Author

Mark Chungmoon Chang, a native of Korea, was the Professor of the New Testament at St. Michael's Anglican Seminary in Seoul, Korea, and is presently the Rector of St. Peter's Episcopal Church, the Diocese of Newark, New Jersey. He studied at Methodist Theological Seminary, Soong Sil University, St. Michael's Anglican Seminary, United Graduate School of Yonsei University (M.Th.) in Seoul, and at General Theological Seminary (S.T.M.), Union Theological Seminary in New York City and earned his Ph.D. from Pacific Western University in Los Angeles.

He published Korean translations of *Born of A Woman* by Roger Tennant, and of *Korean Days and Works* by Richard Rutt.

Married to Esther Haing-Im, the Changs have two grown daughters and one son.

CONTENTS

Chapter IV

PART II: ANALYTICAL EXPOSITION

Chapter V

Chapter VI

FOREWORD

I wish to commend very warmly this book by the Rev. Dr. Mark Chang. During the entire period of the development of modern theology, from Schleiermacher onward, the question of hermeneutics or the science of interpretation has been attracting attention, and it is impossible to get very far in theology without facing this issue. What is the meaning of the Bible for people living so many centuries after it was composed? Indeed, more fundamentally, what does it mean to talk of God at all?

Especially in the past few decades, both philosophers and theologians have devoted much of their effort to these difficult questions. The result is a vast literature, to which such famous scholars as Heidegger, Bultmann, Gadamer, Ebeling, Ricoeur and many others have made important contributions.

Dr. Chang has done much patient research into this wide and difficult area of study. He has familiarized himself with the different standpoints, and offers perceptive judgments on their strengths and weaknesses. He has now published the results of his work, and his book will be a most valuable resource to those who want to get to grips with the important questions which it discusses.

University of Oxford   John Macquarrie

PREFACE

The peculiar character of Chinese writing has left an indelible stamp on the nature of thought throughout East Asia. Because wrting began as pictography, later abstract concepts remained firmly rooted in the concrete situations originally portrayed by the character. Thus the word *tao*, a term akin to the Greek *logos*, denoting the order of the universe, began as a simple picture of a path or road. The basic meaning of the character remains, alongside the philosophical use, to this day. Of course, this concrete-abstract nature of words exists in most languages as well. But the Western system of spelling, itself an abstraction, cannot exhibit the same *visual* tie to the material base possessed by Chinese.

Consequently, although Dr. Chang has written an extremely interesting essay in Biblical interpretation based mainly on a critical survey of European and North American sources, his conclusions (it seems to me) have been shaped by his own roots, as a Korean convert to Christianity, in East Asian civilization. In working toward a method of interpretation he surveys the outstanding contributions of British, German and North American scholarship to hermeneutics, based on myth and symbol. He finds all of them valuable but wanting. Some, like Bultmann, "are more concerned with the existential *content* of myth," while "the exponents of symbolic interpretation are likewise too concerned with the symbolic form (or expression)." In contrast, Chang calls for a mediating position which would treat the whole in its "organic unity", and he proceeds to develop his own method of "logical empiricism".

In effect, it is in this emphasis on a holistic method, grounded on linguistic analysis (particularly in this essay on the analysis of spatial and temporal language in the New Testament), that the author reveals his roots in East Asian culture. No abstract methodological theory can do the job that a study of the words themselves can produce. Moreover, as a pastor and preacher, the communication of the Gospel to ordinary people within the context of contemporary society comes first. This, too, involves a holistic approach to the interpretation of scripture as part of the life and liturgy of the believing community. Thus a process that began as an academic and critical analysis ends as a call to practical action.

I enjoyed reading Dr. Chang's essay from beginning to end. The argument, though highly compressed and allusive, remains lucid throughout. It was easy to follow, even for a non-specialist like myself, for whom the critical survey at the beginning became an introduction to the literature of biblical hermeneutics. The critique of Bultmann and Tillich seemed particularly cogent, while the argument for action at the conclusion of the essay appealed strongly to one concerned with the liberation movements of the Third World. We can thank Dr. Chang for performing a useful and important task, and we hope that many will be able to take advantage of his study.

Trinity College
University of Toronto

Cyril H. Powles
Emeritus Professor
History of Christianity

AKNOWLEDGEMENTS

The substance of the present work, which has since been revised, was submitted as a Ph.D. dissertation to Pacific Western University, Los Angeles. I wish to express my deep thanks to my examiners, Professor Simeon Wade, Ph.D. and Professor Herbert W. Haberland, Ph.D. for their commendations and valuable suggestions, which I have adopted.

This hermeneutical study has grown out of much academic inspiration, encouragement, and much personal support from many people.

A special debt of gratitude is due to Dr. John Macquarrie, Lady Margaret Professor of Divinity, University of Oxford, for writing such a generous Foreword to the book. Professor Macquarrie taught and encouraged me at General Theological Seminary and Union Theological Seminary in New York City from 1969 to 1970. His philosophical theology and its existential-ontological language have influenced my work.

I am deeply grateful to Dr. Cyril H. Powles, Emeritus Professor of Trinity College, University of Toronto, for reading the dissertation and commending it as well as writing the Preface. His valuable advice has given me further hermeneutical insights.

My warm thanks are due also to the Right Reverend Vicars Short, D.D., the former Diocesan Bishop of Saskatchewan and once Acting Dean, Trinity College, University of Toronto, for lending his enthusiastic support.

I will always be profoundly aware of the foundation of my interest in hermeneutics given to me by the late Professor Yong Ok Kim, Ph.D. It was he who first taught and encouraged me in the New Testament and its hermeneutics at Methodist Theological Seminary and the United Graduate School of Theology, Yonsei University, in Seoul, Korea. I regret that he is not able to read this book.

I should like also to express my sincere thanks to Professor Harold H. Sunoo, Ph.D. of Central Methodist College in Missouri, for his comments and encouragement; and Professor Dong Soo Kim, Ph.D. of Norfolk State University in Virginia; and Dr. Sook Ja Paik, Ph.D. of Heritage Research House, Inc., for their technical supports and editorial advice in my undertaking to publish this work.

Finally, I am so thankful to the Right Reverend Paul C. Lee, D.D., LL.D., C.B.E., the former Senior Bishop of the Anglican Church in Korea and presently the Chairman of the Board Directors of Yonsei University; the Late Dr. & Mrs. James W. Gramling, M.D., Gadsden, Alabama; the Rev. Harold Voelkel, D.D. who was a Presbyterian missionary in Korea; the Rev. Dr. Roger Tennant, Ph.D., England; my parents; Esther, my wife; and my children, Hilda, Luke, and especially Christina, who all have supported my academic work and life with continuing prayers, wishes, financial contributions and labours.

MacDowall, Saskatchewan   Mark C.M. Chang
Canada   1987

PART I: CRITICAL CONTEXT

This part will deal with the problem and methodology of the thesis. The methodology here is especially important because it is to be understood as the contextual identification of this thesis. The methodology includes existential interpretation and symbolic interpretation, and also a third type of interpretation, by which we mean a mediating position, which draws merits and advantages from the first two. This thesis mainly follows the third method, which is an analytical method of linguistic symbolism.

Chapter I

Introduction: The Problem and Method

This book is intended as a study of the semantic and hermeneutical problem of New Testament language, particularly its language of space and time.

Today, one of the central concerns in theology and biblical study is the interest in linguistics and hermeneutics. Without an adequate knowledge of language and hermeneutical theory, it is impossible to do any genuine scientific study for biblical and theological problems. A further important thing to note here is that the linguistic and hermeneutical study inevitably involves modern philosophical concepts and methodologies. Without understanding modern philosophical terms and analytical method, we cannot interpret the Bible adequately.

Nevertheless, there are still many Christian teachers and preachers who are not interested in or who do not know anything about modern biblical hermeneutics. They often do not realize the serious problems their a-hermeneutical teachings and preachings can cause in their churches, societies and world. We know how the conservative dogmatic teaching of the traditional churches and the fundamentalist reading of the sectarian Protestants have distorted the meaning of the biblical text. They both are very different in the content of teaching, yet they have a common factor in guarding against any new hermeneutical search. They are both suspicious of the philosophical entanglement of modern biblical

3

hermeneutics, and insist on their traditional, or fundamentalist, way of teaching. As Anthony Thiselton indicated,[1] the classical example of such anti-philosophical trend is found in the Church Father Tertullian, who distrusted philosophy as a source of truth, and its modern form is seen in Helmut Thielicke's criticism of Rudolf Bultmann: "Whenever a non-biblical principle derived from contemporary secular thought is applied to the interpretation of the Bible, the Bible's *facultas se ipsum interpretandi* is violated with fatal results. This is what happened in Kant's philosophy, and again in theological idealism. It is happening in Bultmann too."[2]

However, the problem here is that these conservative or anti-philosophical groups often do not realize their indebtedness to certain philosophical traditions. Tertullian was under the influence of Stoic philosophy and tried to use that philosophy as a tool. This is also true of Thelicke when he tries to argue away Bultmann's anti-historicity of the *Kerygmatic* event. His emphasis on the historicity of the *Kerygma* is under the influence of nineteen century historicism. Even the literalism of fundamentalist faith is also based on its own pseudo-scientific philosophy when they insist that Genesis story can be proved scientifically. All this means that any position of biblical interpretation cannot be independent of certain philosophical or outside influence whether the interpreter realizes this or not. The reason for this is that, unless it is an extremely fanatical or mystical religion, all religious and theological interpreters try to appeal to the logic of human mind. Thus, the important thing to admit here is that the anti-philosophical or anti-intellectual arguments are, in fact, not against the use of philosophy, but against any particular kind of philosophy. This implies that an adequate philosophical tool is useful and necessary for biblical hermeneutics.

The importance of hermeneutics and its philosophical involvement, I believe, can be traced back to Jesus, who was the original exponent of new biblical interpretation. The writer of St. Mark's Gospel says that "The people who heard him were amazed at the way he taught. He was not like the teacher of the Law; instead, he taught with authority." (MK 1:22). What then was his new teaching and what kind of method did he use in his new teaching? In a word, his teaching was about the depth reality of human life, and his method of teaching was the use of popular imagery or symbolic language so that its meaning could be meaningfully and powerfully communicated to his audience. His keen insight into human life was grounded upon his deep faith in God's revealing love, and his powerful language was due to his hermeneutical genius, which the Lucan Gospel suggests in introducing Jesus' childhood.

We believe that this is the biblical ground of the new hermeneutics which involves philosophical understanding. When we say this, the question may be asked of how can we regard the preaching or teaching of Jesus, the Nazareth carpenter, as a philosophical kind of teaching or method? However, before asking this question, the meaning of the word, philosophy, should be re-examined here. If the word philosophy is to be used only for the purely intellectual or rational category of thought and mind, the living or personal and practical knowledge of the Hebrew-Christian tradition might be classified as another category, one distinct from the classical Greek philosophy and western intellectualism. However, the notion or meaning of the word, philosophy, today has become very different from its traditional understanding. William Halverson says in his book, *A Concise Introduction to Philosophy* that "Philosophy means a general view of life, or a general theory about how one ought to go about the living of one's life." Here, too "philosophy is understood to have a very practical orientation...but includes the whole of life."[3] In this sense we can say that Jesus's keen insight into human life and its transcendent reality is of the greatest hermeneutical and philosophical significance.

Philosophy today has been expanded enough to include the knowledge of person and life. The rationalism of the Enlightenment or positivistic logical empiricism is no longer influential. The new emphasis on the human reality is also shown in distinguished modern philosophers: Karl

Popper's and Michael Polanyi's epistemology, and particularly in Polanyi's epistemology which stresses a personal dimension of knowledge. Professor Macquarrie
writes that "it is Polanyi who brings out in detail the personal contribution to and participation in the act of
knowledge."[4] Macquarrie himself emphasizes that "the
cognitive or intellective activities have to be set in the
broader spectrum of personal existence."[5]

This new aspect of modern philosophy means that adequate philosophical study today cannot be independent of
theological subjects which deal with life and its ultimate
meaning. This is also true of the other pole of modern
philosophy, that is, biblical and theological study, which
cannot be independent of philosophical concept and
methodology. For this reason, in this century, the new
trend of philosophical theology or theological philosophy,
if we can call the latter so, are particularly apparent. R.
Bultmann, Paul Tillich, J. Macquarrie and others can be
called philosophical theologians by their use of
philosophical concepts as methodological tools. Cassirer,
Urban, Heidegger, Gadamer, P. Ricoeur and others can be
regarded as religious or theological philosophers although
most of them might reject such an imposing title.

The above statements are to show that theology and
philosophy are inter-dependent particularly through their
hermeneutical areas. Now, we can turn to the more
specific problem of modern biblical hermeneutics.

Modern hermeneutical and semantic problems begin
with Rudolf Bultmann's Demythologizing (*Entmythologisierung*) which brought a Copernican revolution in the history of modern biblical 'hermeneutics.'
There have been many books written surrounding the subject as either a controversial problem or as a great contribution. The important aspect of his Demythologizing
program has been the question of meaning attached to the
word, 'hermeneutics.[6] H.P. Owen has said that
Bultmann's theology "is an attempt to discover the meaning of the New Testament."[7] No doubt today our primary
concern, as Professor John Macquarrie writes, is the ques-

tion of the meaning and the problem of communication, and this is logically prior to the question of truth which formerly the Christian apologist tried to demonstrate.[8]

However, the problem today has become more sophisticated than ever. That is a further question: What is the meaning itself? This semantic question involves our hermeneutical questions: What is the meaning of the biblical text?, How is the text defined? How can we understand it? What is the understanding of the text? What is its interpretation?

Before discussing these questions, let us introduce the linguistic situation of the modern world, and the procedure of the present study. As modern devices make the world smaller and smaller, we find ourselves under the necessity of mastering more foreign tongues. But the more serious problem of communication lies in our own language, because today familiar words have lost their meaning for many. This is even more true of communication within the Christian Church today. If this problem is not solved, our preaching is, as Amos N. Wilder said, like speaking into a dead microphone.[9]

With this account of the general problem about the present hermeneutic questions as a background, we can reduce our discussion to the main concern of this thesis, that is, spatio-temporal language in the New Testament mythological language. We found that, although there has been much serious discussion about theological and biblical hermeneutic problems, a main point of the matter has been overlooked by many scholars. We should say that it is the question of space and time language in the New Testament mythology which demands proper understanding in terms of the new hermeneutics. But as we know, Bultmann is a stern critic of the spatio-temporal conception of language in the New Testament mythology,[10] although he suggests the possibility of an existential interpretation of it. Nevertheless, we have reason to give a positive answer to this question of the language. In order to do this we would attach importance to analysis of the symbolic language and its meaning.

Our method of developing the thesis can be illustrated as below:

CRITICAL CONTEXT

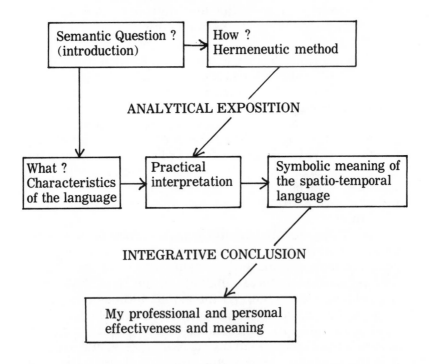

Diagram 1

As seen in this diagram, our study begins with a question about the meaning of the given language, and proceeds to two subsequent questions: that of the methodological question of the interpretation, and that of determining the characteristics of the spatio-temporal language. We should know that these two questions and their treatment are of great importance, because the final answer to our semantic question is to be decided according to the consequences of the treatment of these two questions. But we must have a further intermediary step, that is, practical interpretation which means its application in a given text. When we have fully discussed these questions, we reach the final answer.

In dealing with the methodological question, we will critically examine the consequences of contemporary discussions about two types of interpretations, that is, existential interpretation and symbolic interpretation, and also a third type of interpretation, by which we mean a linguistic and hermeneutical approach in which linguistic symbolism and its spatio-temporal semantics[11] are discussed. But before examining the above interpretations, a general view of modern hermeneutical problems and methodological proposals for the solutions will be surveyed.

The question of deciding the characteristics of mythological language will be dealt with in Chapter V. And in Chapters VI and VII, there will be a practical hermeneutic attempt made with linguistic analysis of the texts by which the symbolic structure of the space and time language can be shown. Then the meaning of the language can be understood by us who aim to find its modern relevance. This interpretation will be presented with three divisions of space and time language, respectively, spatial, temporal, and spatio-temporal language. These correspond to the three storied universe as the cosmological, the *parousia* as the eschatological, and the ascension story as the Christological myth.

The interpretation of the given language brings out the symbolic structure of space and time language in the New Testament text, and shows its spiritual and universal meanings which meet us through the hermeneutical process. Our emphasis on space and time language is that space and time imagery is the prime experience of finite human life, and this experience accompanies the ultimate value dimension of human existence. This fact is particularly true of religious language, and is much more true of Christian life, because our ultimate concern is to attain to that spaceless and timeless transcendent reality, which, in New Testament faith, would be revealed in Christ's redemptive act, especially in his Exaltation expressed in the images of the risen Christ, his Ascension and his sitting at the right hand of God in heaven.   This Exaltation language is to stress the trans-spatial and trans-temporal dimension of God's redemptive act and its revealing power.

God's redemptive act includes the dimension of space and time in terms of his Incarnation, his historical life, suffering and death.   This dimension of His redemptive act is to expose the negative reality of spatio-temporal situation, and to inspire His people to see beyond the spatio-temporal boundaries to the trans-space and trans-time reality, which is expressed as the heavenly eternal Home. But this should not be misunderstood as a hermeneutical support or comfort to any escapist faith and after-death religion which ignores, or is not responsible for, the present reality of our spatio-temporal life.   The triumphant story of Christ's Ascension is not to comfort the escapist faith, but to stress the meaning of overcoming the spatio-temporal situations in the wider context of spatio-temporal and trans-spatio-trans-temporal dimensions.   In God's creation or his universe, there are no any boundaries. Only finite human experience and language give us such knowledge. The important thing which the trans-spatial and trans-temporal language of the risen and ascended Christ reveals is the dynamic character of the saving story. That is why the Ascension stories of Christ often accompany imperative language together with the indicative and promise languages.   Christian life as Christ's discipleship means to follow Jesus Christ and participate in his spatio-trans-spatio and his temporal-trans-temporal redemptive act. The resurrection and Ascension stories are characterized by a mission charge. The disciples of Jesus Christ are described in the resurrection-Ascension stories as sent to the world to witness to Him, and to transform the world. They are also told to pray that your kingdom come, your will be done, on earth as in heaven.

Our conclusion to the book is where we restate the spiritual and symbolic meaning of the space and time language in our professional and personal experiences. Symbolic meaning is to be communicated effectively to us and is intelligible only when it is the personal expression of our lived experience.

A.   Methodological Question of Modern Interpretation of New Testament Mythology

Insofar as our main question is concerned in the hermeneutic problem, the methodological question of dealing with this problem is inevitable. Therefore the purpose of this chapter is to consider the contemporary discussion of methological problems of interpreting New Testament mythological language. In doing so, we shall know what is the appropriate method of its interpretation.

As is well known, many books have been written about this subject, and various attempts have been made to solve the problem of interpretation. Nevertheless, the problem remains still unsolved. Now let us begin with a discussion of the nature of the problem.

We should first of all admit with Bultmann that the message of salvation in the New Testament, the *kerygma* of the New Testament, is wrapped up or expressed in a mythological form, that is in mythological language, which presents a considerable number of problems to the hearer of the present day. For instance, expressions like "he descended into hell" or "he ascended into heaven" or "he will come from heaven at the last day", can not have any significant meaning for us, insofar as the literal sense of the space and time language is not modified through our interpretation. Here, then, the question arises --what kind of interpretation is appropriate to the space and time language? In later paragraphs, we will discuss all these

problems. Bultmann said that the liberal theologians of
the last century sought to eliminate the shell and expose
the kernel, for the shell seemed to them the antiquated
mythology, and the kernel supposedly an idealistic
humanitarian and religious ethic. But their attempt to
solve the problem resulted in eliminating the *kerygma*
itself, the message of God's saving act in Christ.[12]

The successor in academic circles, called the History
of Religion school, who tried to understand Christianity not
as just ethical idealism but as piety and a cultus, also
eliminated the act of God. Here the question of the famous
Entmythologisierung of Bultmann arises. As he writes,
"whereas the older liberals used criticism to eliminate
(*elimiert*) the mythology of the New Testament, our task
today is to use criticism to interpret (*interpretieren*) it."[13]
This is a key work about resolving the mythological
language. Is this right? We will presently investigate his
method of interpretation and examine what his interpretation does actually mean. But it can be said that, despite his
great contribution to contemporary understanding of interpretation, his method of interpretation also is subjected
to another criticism. That is why we must go beyond his
Demythologizing to a new way of the interpretation, that
is, the third method of interpretation which deals mostly
with linguistic symbolism, and hermeneutical truth.

B.   General View of Modern Hermeneutical
      Theories

Let us then survey the further problems of modern
hermeneutics and suggest the possible solution to them.

As we mentioned, the modern hermeneutical problem,
especially the hermeneutical questions raised in the past
few decades are more sophisticated than before. What is
the meaning itself? What is the biblical text and how is it
interpreted and understood? What is the meaning of interpretation or understanding? These questions imply the
need for new hermeneutical theories.[14] Here, the names of

modern hermeneutical philosophers such as Hans-Georg Gadamer and Paul Ricoeur are involved. However, insofar as our spatio-temporal hermeneutics is concerned, Ernst Cassirer's and W. M. Urban's linguistic philosophy is also important.

Bultmann's existentialist hermeneutics has been criticized for its existential prejudice and its anthropocentric onesidedness. The criticism is made not only of the existentialist method. In the light of new hermeneutical theories, the nature or meaning of the text has been critically re-examined. What is the text? Is it to uncover the sense of the text intended by the original writer and understood by the original readers? Does the understanding of a given text mean the knowledge of the sacred author and sharing in the understanding of the audience of the first century? These questions are directed to the historio-critical method of biblical exegesis which has been considered as paradigmatic for biblical research in this century.

The historio-critical method has concerned the historical information about the first century Christian thought and practice for use in the negotiation of current church problems. For instance, the articles of *The Theological Words Book of New Testament* (Theologisches Woerterbuch zum Neuen Testament), *Form Criticism* (Formgeschichte), *Traditio-Historical Criticism* (Ueberlieferungsgeschichte), have their methodological basis in such historical criticisms. Is this a proper exhaustive method? Jesuit scholar Sandra Schneiders indicates that there is "the increasingly vocal discontent of many, within and outside the biblical academy, who, for good reasons and bad, are decrying the religious sterility of much exegetical production."[15] Schneiders believes that the historical criticism is faced with limits

> on two fronts, the philosophical and the literary. On the one hand, the epistemological and ontological questions of what it means to interpret and to understand as opposed to gathering information are being

raised. On the other hand, literary questions regarding the whole range of expressive or symbolic language and the functioning of such megaforms as narrative and such subgenres as parable are emerging.[16]

The historical critical hermeneutics, considered as an exhaustive method, is inadequate for the biblical interpretation in terms of positivistic historicism.

However, this should not mean that a new hermeneutical theory totally denies the role of the historical criticism, which has status as "an indispensable moment in the full interpretative process.[17] How can the dichotomy of the two entities, the fact and value (or meaning) be solved?

In this connection, Bultmannean existential hermeneutics, of which other critical aspects will be dealt with in the following chapter, will be re-examined. The crucial point we want to make here is that existentialist approach is open to a critical question, "What is the meaning of understanding a biblical text?" Wolfhart Pannenberg points out that existentialist interpretation, "like the psychological interpretation of Schleiermacher and Dilthey, also restricts the question about the contemporary significance of the past to that which a transmitted text expresses concerning the question of human existence."[18] The New Testament texts deal with many other subjects than possibilities of understanding human existence. The more important message they express is the understanding of God and of the world for which a further extended horizon of understanding is required, which Pannenberg calls "the horizon of universal history," and philosophers Hans-Georg Gadamer and Paul Ricoeur express in terms of "a fusion of horizons between the world of the reader and the world of the text in the act of appropriation by which the reader openly engages the reference or truth claim of the text, risking his or her own 'world' in the confrontation with the world of the text and surrounding to the truth about the subject matter."[19] However, the problem still remains when the new hermeneutical theories do not raise the question about the value dimension of language, particularly of space and time which should, I believe, be one of the most important subjects in any hermeneutical study. What is the reference or truth of the text? Can we understand the non-ostensive or ideal reality without hermeneutical discussion of the space and time language and its value words?

Let us, then, turn to another hermeneutical movement called "structural analysis" or interpretation. This new approach, which has been made by European literary critics, is still young in terms of its introduction to biblical studies. The structuralism has arisen as a challenge to the above hermeneutical methods, that is, the historical critical methodology and existential hermeneutics. Franqois Bevon describes his point of view on the structuralist methodology of biblical interpretation as the following:

1) Turned too long towards diachrony (cf. the commentaries, the articles of the *Theologishes Woerterbuch zum Neuen Testament*), exegesis will find its bearings in synchrony.
2) Structuralism will serve as a balance to existential analysis. It is an indispensable balance, because the true hermeneutic is an appropriation of meaning. But it is an appropriation of meaning which is possible only if one keeps his distance from the text.[20]

The above description is a brief view of the characteristics of structuralism. Today there are many different views among the structuralists themselves, so that it is not easy to point out what structuralism really is. However, its main characteristic, which is common to them, can be shown here from our perspective.

The emphatic point of structuralism is its synchronic priority over diachronic approach, according to Saussurean tradition. The French linguist Ferdinand de Saussure at the beginning of this century showed that there is, in contrast to the historical method which considered the *langue* in its diachrony (literally: through the time), an interpretation of the *langue*, which he called synchronic (literally: at the same time)...Instead of studying the evolution of one *langue* he (Saussure) preferred to stop and consider the *system* which constitutes that *langue*. Thus he showed...what would come to be of primary importance for structuralism...that the relationships between the terms, which he called the *differences*, are more significant than the isolated terms of language.[21]

In this connection, Roland Barthes' words are worthy to note here. He, one of the main introducers of biblical structuralism, writes, "This textual analysis seeks to 'view' the text in its difference...that does not mean to say in its hidden individuality, because this difference is 'woven' (*tisseé*) in well-known codes, but the text is caught in an *open* net... the infinity itself of the language...which is completely structured."[22]

We do not need any more details about the nature of structuralism in this introductory stage of the present study. The important thing to be pointed out here is the problematic result which the new linguistic and literary movement might bring out in Christian biblical hermeneutics. Its main problem is that the synchronic approach is a self-sufficient linguistic method without relations to external, non-semeiotic reality or truth. According to Paul Ricoeur, the structuralist model fails to see that the language to be interpreted has non-ostensive reference, the kind of world opened up by the depth semantics of the text, a discovery which has immense consequences regarding what is usually called the sense of the text.[23]

Our view on structuralism is that its method is to discover the meaning of biblical text horizontally within and between the functional differences in the same organic system, so to say, just as a medical specialist tries to discover and interpret any occurrence of bodily functions in terms of internal relations. We, of course, admit the psycho-somatic reality of our human living existence, yet there is more than the horizontal system. This further dimension is the ultimate spiritual reality (or mysterious truth) which cannot be confined to any internal organic system.   This is also true of our semantic and hermeneutical methodology. The ultimate meaning of the text cannot be brought out from its synchronic systems. Language as logos is not only *"langue,"* as Saussure himself admits, there is another dimension *"parole"* as an event, which P. Ricoeur prefers to call "discourse." Semantic and hermeneutical ground should be found in this discourse dimension.

However, our criticism of the structural interpretation should not mean that the structural approach does not include any positive contributions. We should recognize the helpful aspects of the analytical method, especially in its handling of narrative texts and discovery of the "actuant" element, which some symbolic oriented New Testament scholars today have tried to apply to the interpretation of the biblical parables like "Good Samaritan."[24] The structural analysis pays more attention to the text, especially the biblical story and understands it as a whole. This is a different method from the traditional historical critical method, which concerns an author, his thought with its dependencies, and his genius.

Ricoeur admits the structural analysis in terms of superstructure, which is a preparatory step to the infrastructure in which the non-ostensive meaning or power can be found. But the structural analysis is not interested in such deep reality. The structuralists think its horizontal synchronic method as a self-sufficient one. However, our view is that the structuralist method is not right as long as it cannot see the further dimension of diachronic and vertical reality. In regards to the cosmological reference, the position of structuralism is not clear. The structuralists mention the importance of the cosmological meaning of the biblical stories, but how can they find out the cosmological meaning?   They use, occasionally, the spatial and temporal terms, yet there is no study of the spatial-temporal semantics. Here, again, without spatio-temporal semantics, and such hermeneutics, we suspect there is not a genuine understanding of the biblical text, especially God's redemptive stories, as shown in Exodus and Christological stories.

Now we can turn to our specific concern, that is the hermeneutical task of the space and time language. However, unfortunately, there are very limited studies in this area. As far as we know, there is almost no such specific study in modern hermeneutical works in spite of the importance of the subject. Any of Heidegger, Bultmann, Gadamer and Wittgenstein, whom Thiselton lists as the most influential hermeneutic thinkers in this century, do not deal with the semantic subject of the space and time language, except in Heidegger's existential analysis of *Dasein* under the title of *Sein und Zeit*, which cannot be regarded as a proper semantics of the space and time language. Some concern and study of this area is found in Paul Tillich's works, but, as it shall be shown in the chapter of symbolic interpretation, he does not deal with any semantic aspect of the specific language.

The real academic clue and resources are sought for in the philosophy of E. Cassirer, W. M. Urban, and Edwyn Bevan, whose main works were done in the earlier part of this century. Their magnificent philosophical and semantic studies include the analysis of space and time language. Here is one of the important words which Urban indicates in presenting the rule of linguistic symbolism. He writes, "Gradually the *Gestalt* is detached from its primary material and becomes the means of intuitive representation of plurality and repetition and finally, in many cases, becomes the form of representation or expression of the fundamental intuitions, space, time, force, etc."[25] These words are of importance in showing how semantic form is developed at the initial level. They also imply that the basic content of semantic meaning is the intuitive element. However, the most interesting and important thing is that language as symbolic form includes space, time and force as its fundamental semantic content of which the study is our main concern. Here, further attention should be paid to the term "force." The dynamic character of language is generally acknowledged by modern linguistic philosophers.   Ricoeur suggests a significant involvement of spatial concept in the force or power when he writes,

> I am inclined to say that what asks to be brought to language in symbols, but which never passes over completely   into language, is always something powerful, efficacious, forceful. Man, it seems, is here designated as a power to exist, indirectly discerned from above, below, and laterally.[26]

This view of the force or power leads him to the dialect between the form and power in his hermeneutic theory. This is one of the reasons he stresses the role of the verb in the subject-predicate structure of sentence, which for him is the semantic unit.[27]

Insofar as linguistic dynamism is concerned, the philosophy of Henry Bergson can be a supporting ground; yet his pure dynamism or activism results in neglecting the logical dimension of language--his position is called a-logical intuitionism. For Bergson, natural language is the misrepresentation or distortion of reality. He indicates the three grammatical categories, nouns, adjectives, and verbs as the ways of seeing things, and disvalues them, particularly the noun and adjective as static. "The only part of speech that expresses reality is the verb, and then only in its aspect of intuitive expression of becoming and transitivity. Nouns and adjectives, essences and qualities, must all be vaporized into verbs.[28] Urban states that, "in such dynamism, distinctions between subject and predicate, and between predicate and activity all break down."

Distinct from this alogical intuism, Urban stresses the third element of semantic structure, that is the adjective value dimension of language. This point is particularly important for our religious language of space and time. As he writes, "On the question of the noun and the verb there is no dispute. Almost all languages make some division between the two parts of a sentence; the only question is as to the third."[29] Philosophers or theologians in the hermeneutics of this century do not say much about the semantic meaning or hermeneutical principle of the space and time language. We think that this absence of the specific study raises a serious question about the integrity of their hermeneutical theories. We doubt that, without semantic and hermeneutical study of the space and time language, their hermeneutic theories can be successful. We believe that any semantic study of language, especially of religious language cannot be independent of space and time relations. Examined closely, all religious languages include the space-time expressions as their key factors. This is especially true of Jewish and Christian writings.

In this connection, W. Urban's linguistic philosophy, especially his work *Language and Reality*, is of great importance for our present study.

We firmly believe that spatial and temporal semantics of biblical language is of the utmost importance and urgency because, when closely examined, the main concern of the biblical text, particularly, *kerygmatic* language, is in the spatial and temporal question--this is also the reality of our general human consciousness. In other words, our consciousness of spatial and temporal finitude is of the most serious and deepest question. This question is expressed in various kinds of language and life: consciousness of empty space and of time transition; the mysterious question to the remote universe, the memory and attachment to the irreversible beautiful past days, and the hope, future, and the world after death. How can we interpret and understand these question? These questions themselves are proof that human life and language are searching for meaningfulness. The empty space should be filled with meaning or value. The consciousness of fleeting time should be filled with qualitative meanings. This means that our spatio-temporal existence, symbolized both as being thrown in the wilderness, and as falling flowers or leaves, wants to overcome the spatio-temporal boundaries and achieve trans-spatial, trans-temporal reality so that we can enjoy the ultimate values expressed as heavenly and eternal. But this is not possible for a spatial and temporal being affected with sin. Here is the reason why the Saviour Christ passed through or over-came the spatio-temporal boundaries. Our New Testament Christology stresses this victorious Saviour so that Christian people can follow their Lord, the pioneer to the heavenly eternal home where light and bliss are symbolic value language.

C.   Proposal for Spatio-Temporal Semantics

However, traditional theology and biblical interpreta-tions have not dealt with spatio-temporal meaning. The lack of spatio-temporal hermeneutical knowledge has resulted in great division and confusion in the Christian world and among theological teachings. Some Christian groups have been criticized for their escapist or "after-death" type of faith, and others have been blamed for modern Sadduceeism or optimist religion. Some others have more interest in existential terms of "here and now," and still others in cosmological or futuristic "there and then." On the one hand, there have been romanist historical hermeneutics which has shown concern in the psychoogy of ancient authors, and on the other hand on new hermeneutics in new horizons of the text. We think that each of these positions has a certain contribution to theological and hermeneutical developments. But their common problem is the lack of spatio-temporal semantics. The traditional and even new hermeneutical theories have not realized how important and serious the spatial and temporal perspective of biblical hermeneutics is. The ultimate reality of faith and life is not to be found in any one sided emphasis. We need both entities, here and there, now and then, depth and height, the past and future, the present world and after death dimension. But the answer to these dichotomies should not be the mere combination or compromising of the two, because human life is moving and becoming total existence. Thus, the dichotomy should be interpreted and understood in terms of dialectic synthesis. What, then, is the factor which makes the synthesis possible? It is the value dimension [30] of our life experience and language. By the value dimension here we mean the quality experience of our personal and social life and its expressions like joy, satisfaction, love, righteousness, light and so on. We find this answer through the examination of the biblical language, especially spatial and temporal language.

In our bible, there are many enriched spatial and temporal terms and imageries, and these often include value words like "light," "holiness, righteousness," "faithfulness," "majesty," "strength," "beauty," "greatness," "splendour," "glory," "power," "delightedness," and so on.

The following are the examples of the usage of these terms: "Everyone will see the Lord's splendor, see his greatness and power" (Is 33:2). "Man's loyalty will reach up from the earth, and God's righteousness will look down from heaven" (Ps 85:10-13). "The Lord rules over all nations: his glory is above the heavens. There is no one like the Lord our God. He lives in the heights above but he bends down to see the heavens and the earth" (Ps 113:4ff). "Who will go up into heaven?" "Who will go down into the world below?" "God's message is near you, on your lips and in your heart" (Rom 10:66-8). "For I am certain that nothing can separate us from his love...neither the present nor the future, neither the world above nor the world below--there is nothing in all creation that will ever be able to separate us from the love of God..." (Rom 8:38ff). "I have been given all authority in heaven and earth. Go, then to all people everywhere...And remember! I will be with you always, to the end of the age" (Matt 28:18ff). "And I saw the Holy city, the new Jerusalem, coming down out of heaven from God...I am the Alpha and the Omega, the beginning and the end" (Rev 21:1ff).

The above quotations are just some examples of the rich spatial, temporal and value words in the Bible. However, it is enough to show how important it is to know the reality of spatial-temporal and value language. The more important thing here is to recognize that the spatial and temporal dichotomy, like here and there, now and then, in other words, the dichotomy of the existential and cosmological dimensions is synthesized through the upward movement of value words.

The value of "light" is universal entity, which is developed and synthesized through both cosmological and existential experiences.   On the one hand, light has transcendent meaning through the "height" imagery of heaven, as experienced in the light images of sun, moon and stars, which have been developed in the cosmological language; on the other, there have been internal light experiences expressed in terms of existential or Gnostic awakening. These two directions are inseparable in terms of total human experience.

God's holiness, majesty or power are other value words which come from our cosmic and existential experiences. The experience of human finitude demands a transcendent ideality of perfect, unshaken majesty and power.   And this implies that our human existence is a helpless and finite being.   We want to have the steadfastness of a mountain or rock, yet we experience the opposite. This is another universal human experience. In our language, there are many different levels of value words which belong to adjective entity. But more important and symbolic value words are found in religious language, which requires spatial and temporal imageries. Thus, value words involve space and time language. Light in the religious sense accompanies the spatial and temporal value words, like "heavenly light," or "eternal light." The words majesty, power, happiness, blessedness are inclusive like "heavenly power and eternal power," "heavenly blessedness and eternal blessedness," and so on. This means that this value dimension is of universal significance. The communication of religious language comes from this value dimension which is universally valid and meaningful.

The value or qualitative dimension of our space and time existence means that our human life demands spiritual, transcendent reality and its universal communication. That is why "heavenly eternal light" is the main symbolism of Christian language. The spatio-temporal images and value contents are of universal human significance. In the west and east, the ancient and future world, the bright stars are always significant. In this sense, the Christmas story of the Magi and the Star is most meaningful in spatio-temporal semantics.

Nevertheless, our philosophical and theological history has often neglected this spatial-temporal value dimension. As we know, the classical Greek philosophers, Kant and other metaphysical philosophers have not been successful in searching for the reality of space and time. They have argued that neither time nor space can be ultimately real. Reality, they think, does not endure through time nor is it subject to the condition of space. This is the shared idea of Plato, Parmenides, and Zeno, which is the root of the negative metaphysics of space and time.

For Immanuel Kant, space and time are intimately connected through "intuition," by which he meant that they are peculiar sorts of particulars. According to this theory, space and time are bound up with particularity, and only what is particular can be real.

Henry Bergson is concerned with the notions of duration and movement, and understands that the time is experienced as continuous. But he thinks that it is only the spatialized time measured by clocks that was taken to have separable parts (minutes, hours, weeks, and so on), and this "public" time was merely conventional. This view is also of a negative kind, which devalues the meaning of our temporal and spatial consciousness.[31]

The view on space and time is also expressed by the Christian thinker and theologian Paul Tillich. He is right when he says that "Existing means being finite or being in time and space. This holds true of everything in our world."[32] But he makes a serious mistake when he treats time and space as struggling forces, which is a kind of 'spatio-temporal dualism.' He thinks that the space concept belongs to a pagan or negative category while time and historical consciousness is of Judaic Christian character. He says, "Synagogue and church should be united in our age, in the struggle for the God of time against the gods of space."[33] Tillich's view on space and time, of which further discussion will be in the chapter of symbolical interpretation,[34] is existentialism of time priority, which often tends to the forcible conceptualization of abstract notion.

As we have already shown, biblical and Christian spatio-temporal knowledge is of real and experiential character. The biblical writers and Christians vividly imagine the heavenly city or eternal home through their practical experience of earthly Jerusalem or the Temple. And this expression includes inward and outward value dimensions, in other words, existential and cosmological dimensions.

The above discussions are a brief survey of hermeneutical problems. How can the problems be solved? There is no easy answer to this question. Particularly the question about the hermeneutical problem is not to be coupled or answered in particular time and space because it involves ever-increasing new horizons of interpretation. In this connection, Gadamer's term "fusion of horizons"[35] has more relevance to today's philosophical and theological discussion of hermeneutics than traditional ones do. This means that our hermeneutical task calls for the dialectic of ever continuing questions and answers so that a more relevant and rich understanding of the text may be possible. This also means negatively that the traditional romantic hermeneutics of the Schleiermacher-Dilthey tradition, which tried to get inside another person, that is the original writer, and the original addressees has a serious problem. Gadamer says, "...understanding is not based on 'getting inside' another person, on the immediate fusing of one person in another. To understand what a person says is to agree about the object, not to get inside another person and relive his experiences."[36] Gadamer also says that "understanding is certainly not concerned with understanding historically, ie. reconstructing the way in which the text has come into being. Rather, one is understanding the text itself."[37] This means that the text has its own status called semantic autonomy. In other words, the text is detached from both the original writer and from the situation of the original addressees, and has a life of its own. "What is fixed in writing has raised itself publicly into a sphere of meaning in which everyone who can read has an equal share."[38] This view on the text is shared with P. Ricoeur, who believes that "writing creates a new kind of being, a being which originated in an event, the act of composition, but which perdures as ideal meaning, that is, as meaning liberated from its original event and capable of being reactualized in new ways in subsequent events of understanding."[39]

When applied to our biblical hermeneutics, this semantic autonomy leads us to understand what the Gospel testimony means, in other words, to allow the text to become the word of God in the community of believers. S. Schneiders says, "Here the question is not, for example, to establish factually whether Mary Magdalene actually appears in John's Gospel as an apostle in the technical sense of the term but to understand what the Easter proclamation 'I ascend to my Father and your Father, to my God and your God' (John 20:17) really means."[40]

Insofar as the semantic independence of the text and its semantic fusion with the new horizon of an interpreter are concerned, there is, we believe, no question. Many literary or religious writers say that their writings have often been read or understood by their readers in different terms of meaning from their original intention. Nevertheless, the writings or the text are meaningful to their readers. This means that the readers or interpreters have their own concerns and pre-understanding when they read or interpret their texts.

Now we have some questions of Gadamer's and Ricoeur's hermeneutic theories, especially in connection with our subject, that is the interpretation of space and time language. In spite of the great popularity of these theories in the philosophical or theological world, their works do not include the hermeneutical subject of the spatial and temporal language, which, we believe, has crucial importance in any hermeneutical task.

Here our attention is drawn to W. Urban's value language, which is indebted to Cassirer and E. Husserl's phenomenological terms "Gestalt" and "intention." These give us some methodological suggestions to pursue our spatio-temporal hermeneutics of the New Testament.

As to Urban's value language, we are interested in his discussions of adjectival entity in addition to the noun and the verb as basic parts of sentence structure. The adjective entity which has more intuitive meaning and power belongs to value dimension in human life in which the spatial and temporal existence finds its paramount expression. Our personal life is perpetually haunted by a sense of meaninglessness or empty feeling, and this means that our life is perpetually pursuing some more ultimate values. This is particularly true of religious life and its spatio-temporal language.

The main stories in the Christian Bible are the language about filling the empty space and time with meaningful events and values. The story about the Exodus is filled with miracles which overcome the spatio-temporal conditions (crossing of Red Sea, spring water, Manna in the wilderness, Fire cloud, Mt. Sinai and theophany, etc.) so that they could pass through the forty years of the wilderness. The Christological spatio-temporal scheme, that is, the pre-existence of Christ, his descending (Incarnation), and Ascending (exultation) are the saving events or movements which fill the empty space and time or suffering spatio-temporal situations with qualitative values. This means that our world and life without the saviour Jesus Christ are like the barren desert and miserable days. The empty space and time should be filled with light and joy, marching and hope. That is why Christ passed through the desert as the pioneer and showed us the victorious way. Our Christian Bible is more meaningful and communicable when we realize the spatio-temporal meaning of our human existence.

Husserl's "Gestalt" and "intention" can be used as the methodological ground of our semantic search in terms of a structural formula, "the form and content." We believe that "Gestalt" and "intention" are two inseparable semantic entities which interplay to produce their synthetical meaning. The internalized form functions effectively and the intentional outward movement universalizes or communicates the value dimension, which finds paramount expression in religious language, especially space and time language. This inward and outward process, which is the interplay of the form and content, we believe, is a dialectic and qualitative synthesis. Further details about this will be dealt with in Chapter IV, Section C.

So far, we have discussed the general hermeneutical problems of today and the importance of spatial and temporal perspectives in biblical interpretation. Against this general background, let us begin our search for a more specific problem.

Modern biblical hermeneutics began with the famous term "demythologizing" (Entmythologisierung) which was raised in 1941 with the delivery and circulation in mimeograph form of Dr. Bultmann's essay, "Neues Testament und Mythologie."[41] For theological or biblical scholars, the term and the controversy surrounding Bultmann's "demythologizing" may sound one generation old, yet it still remains a key factor in understanding the modern biblical hermeneutical problem. We know how seriously the problem has been discussed in the modern theological world. This hermeneutic program was first a challenge against traditional and dogmatic understanding of New Testament mythological language. Then it has a great impact on theology in general and philosophical arguments as well. The famous controversy between R.

Bultmann and philosopher Karl Jaspers is an example. To quote one of Jasper's answer directed to Bultmann,

> Bultmann's views on the demythologizing of religion, which have aroused widespread and lively discussions, have assumed the proportions of an event touching the very essence of religion. This alone is enough to shake the philosopher out of his aloofness, even though the question is outside his field. But there is more. Bultmann's ideas evolve within the sphere of philosophy and hence are subject to philosophical criticism.[42]

Another important and interesting impact is on Roman Catholic scholars who had not been liberated from traditional Thomistic dogma. Sandra Schneiders, a Jesuit scholar, admits that "Few of these scholars (Roman Catholic) had had the opportunity to come to grips seriously with the Kantian epistemological revolution, much less with the emergence of phenomenology through the work of Hegel, Husserl, and Heidegger. In other words, Catholic biblical scholars were hermeneutically equipped with a nineteenth-century historist methodology operating within the framework of a pre-critical Aristotelian epistemology. It was not until Bultmann unveiled his program of demythologization that the hermeneutical question was reopened in all seriousness."[43]

The importance of Bultmann's demythologizing is still recognized in recent philosophical hermeneutics. Philosopher Hans-Georg Gadamer critically reassesses Bultmann's work in a wider philosophical context.[44] Gadamer, despite raising the critical question about Bultmann's force-understanding (pre-understanding), admits that in New Testament studies, the work of Bultmann on hermeneutics cannot be ignored.

Then we will turn to the problem of existentialist interpretation of Bultmann and his followers. This problem will be discussed in connection with our main purpose of the present work.

Chapter II

Existential Interpretation and Space and Time Language

A.   Bultmann's Demythologizing

When we speak about existential interpretation of biblical message, we know that its exponent is Rudolf Bultmann. What, then, is his existential interpretation? In order to understand it, his conception of mythology should be examined. According to Bultmann, the real intention of myth is to express "a certain understanding of human existence. It believes that the world and human life have their ground and limits in a power which is beyond all that we can calculate or control."[1] This means that, to Bultmann, the myth is a mode of expression for "man's understanding of himself in the world, in which he lives."[2] The problem Bultmann raises here is that mythical imagery and language could be and have been understood as an objective description of the world, which belongs to a scientific function in its analysis of reality structure. Bultmann defines myth in the following statement: "Mythology is the use of imagery to express the other-worldly in terms of this world and the divine in terms of human life, the other side in terms of this side."[3]

This definition of mythology implies that mythology is a very imperfect instrument, and thus demands that mythology be demythologized in non-mythical and non-objective terms, that is, in terms of significance for my existence.   Bultmann believes that this kind of critical understanding has begun in the New Testament itself, especially in the Pauline epistles and St. John's Gospel. For instance, in St. Paul's epistle, "man is sometimes regarded as a cosmic being, sometimes as an independent 'I' for whom decision is a matter of life or death."[4]

Then let us examine Bultmann's existential interpretation for men today. He says that, in the New Testament, there are two kinds of self-understanding contrasted: life outside of faith, and life in faith. The human life outside of faith which is expressed in such mythological terms as sin, flesh, fear (anxiety) or death, means, in demythologized and existentialist terms, life in bondage to tangible, visible realities which, since they are perishing, drag man down to perdition with them. Life in faith, on the other hand, means abandoning the adherence to visible realities, and openness to the forgiving grace of God. This means that, when we live in Christian faith, we are released from our past and opened to God's future. Bultmann says that this is true eschatological existence which has to be constantly renewed via decision and obedience.

In this existentialist interpretation of mythological language, Bultmann makes use of Martin Heidegger's terminology, that is, inauthentic and authentic existence. It has been well known that Bultmann's theology, especially his existentialist interpretation and its hermeneutic methodology are under the influence of Heidegger's existential analytic shown in the book, *Sein und Zeit.* [5]

Yet there is a crucial difference between Bultmann and Heidegger. The secular philosopher assumes that the transition from inauthentic existence is something man can achieve for himself; but, in Bultmann's interpretation of the New Testament, only God's redemptive act can effect this transition from inauthentic to authentic existence.

Is this concept not another mythology?   Bultmann believes that "to speak of God as acting is to speak analogically."[6] According to Bultmann, this manner of speaking involves the events of personal existence, and the encounter with God can be an event for man only here and now within the limits of space and time. In this sense, by his analogical expression 'to speak of God as acting' Bultmann means that "we are confronted with God, addressed, asked, judged or blessed by God."[7]

Now let us examine his demythologized interpretation which is sampled in the two central elements in the Christ event, the cross and the resurrection. He interprets the cross not as an event external to us, but as one which takes place within our own existence. In other words, the cross means our being crucified with Christ. As to the resurrection, he interprets it as a mythological way of proclaiming the Cross's saving significance. This means that the resurrection is not the historical occurrence in the sense of the objective word, but an existential event which takes place in ourselves when the Christ event is preached and received in our faith as the eschatological event.

B.   Existential Interpretation of the Space and
        Time Language

In the above paragraphs, we have outlined the general meaning of Bultmann's demythologizing. Now our main concern, the problem of spatio-temporal language, should be dealt with.

As already mentioned, Bultmann is very critical of and negative towards the spatio-temporal concept and its language, because it is mythical and objectified language which, in principle, misrepresents the reality. He, therefore, demands non-objective and non-mythological interpretation of the spatio-temporal terms which means the use of terms of significance for my existence. Let us examine a few examples of his demythologized and existential interpretation of spatio-temporal language.

Bultmann says that the biblical imagery 'God has domicile in heaven' is mythological, and its meaning is that God is beyond the world, that He is transcendent. The reason for such a crude expression of immense spatial distance is that the primitive thinking "was not yet capable of forming the abstract idea of transcendence."[8] This is also true of the conception of hell, which means the idea of the transcendence of evil as the tremendous power which again and again afflicts mankind. "The location of hell and men whom hell has seized is below the earth in darkness because darkness is tremendous and terrible to men."[9]

As in the meaning of heaven, the idea of the transcendence of God is also imagined by means of the category of time. However, it is not simply the idea of transcendence as such, but of the importance of the transcendence of God, who is never present as a familiar phenomenon, but who is always the coming God, who is veiled by the unknown future.[10]

The above examples may be enough to show what Bultmann's way is of interpreting spatio-temporal language. Now we turn to another important aspect of Bultmann's demythologizing, his hermeneutic methodology.

In a word, Bultmann's demythologizing, as he himself declares, is a hermeneutic method, that is, a method of interpretation, of exegesis.[11] Without knowing this methodology, we can hardly understand the whole structure and meaning of his demythologizing program. In addition, it is necessary to note that the structure of the methodological principles is under the influence of Martin Heidegger's hermeneutic method.[12]

The Right Question

Bultmann's hermeneutic method starts with the proper, adequate formulation of the questions which we ask of the text. He believes that, before we bring forward any answer, we must make sure that we have put our questions with regard to the intention of the text. Otherwise, our interpretation can distort the meaning of the text. For instance, some people believe that the Bible can give answers to the questions about the beginning of the universe, but today it is generally recognized that the Bible cannot supply us with such scientific information. The Bible is primarily a religious book. This means that, to approach the meaning of the Bible, we have to ask religious questions of it. What, then, is the religious question? Is it not a question about God? Yet Bultmann says that "the question which is appropriate to the Bible is the question about human existence,"[13] -- a question to which I am driven by the question which exercises me *existentiell* way, the question of my own existence. For Bultmann, the religious question about God is always the question of God in relation to the questioner's own existence. Personal or individual meaning is emphasized here. That is why the German word 'existentiell' is used.   In this sense, Bultmann makes an assertion: "the question of God and the question of myself are identical."[14] For man's life is moved by the search for God because it is always moved, consciously or unconsciously, by the question about his own personal existence. Then, is there not a danger of prejudging the content of the answer to be elicited from the text? But according to Bultmann, this is not the case. He says that "there is a difference in principle between presuppositions in respect of results and presuppositions in respect of method. It can be said that method is nothing other than a kind of questioning, a way of putting questions."[15]

Then, let us ask what the methodological presupposition of the hermeneutics means. This question brings us to our next topic, that is, the prior-understanding.

Vorverstaendniss -- prior understanding (or pre-understanding). When we approach the text with the hermeneutic question, we have certain concepts or notions about the text. For instance, to understand music, musical interest or experience of the interpreter is presupposed.

Bultmann calls this 'life relation' to the subject-matter in the text. "Without such a relation and such previous understanding -(*Vorverstaendniss*), it is impossible to understand any text."[16] Professor J. Macquarrie interprets this relation as "a certain community of interest between the text and the person who is seeking to understand it."[17] What, then, is the prior understanding which is relevant for eliciting the meaning of the Bible? According to Bultmann, the prior understanding is the understanding which we already have of our own existence.

The Bible came out of the ancient world which had an outlook vastly different from the modern world. We may also say that the Bible contains a divine revelation of matters not accessible to our natural human understanding. Nevertheless, at least the Bible deals with human or existential situations which we can share. A divine Word can be understood by a human hearer. Bultmann applies this principle of prior understanding to those for whom the interpretation is being provided.

In interpretation, there are at least two tasks to be performed. The first is to grasp adequately the meaning of the text being interpreted. The second is to convey that meaning intelligibly to those who are asking for the interpretation. The interpreter has a mediating function. The formulation of the right question which we already discussed is our responsibility to the text. The prior understanding is the other side of the interpreter's responsibility. This responsibility to convey the interpreted meaning of the text to modern man is connected with the prior understanding. Bultmann's interpretation of this function   comes from his conviction that there is something which is already within the range of experience of those he is addressing. The biblical text may be foreign to contemporary man, but at least he can begin to understand what is being talked about when it is a question of human existence or self-understanding. Contemporary man is very much interested in the meaning of his own existence.

Professor Macquarrie explains the above two factors of Bultmann's hermeneutical method, that is, the right question and prior understanding, in connection with "a threefold schema of Reformed exegesis--*explicatio, meditatio,* and *applicatio.* "[18] The *explicatio* has to do with the historical and philological research of the text, and the *applicatio* has to do with putting into practice the teaching of the text. The former is vital if one is to have a responsible and intelligent relation to the text and the latter is equally vital if religion is to make a difference in life.

What, then, is the *meditatio* ? According to Professor Macquarrie this is a hidden process at the heart of interpretation whereby the ancient text can become something meaningful on which someone can act here and now. The hidden process might be understood as a mystery, or the inward testimony of the Holy Spirit. But this account of the matter is not adequate, because the understanding of the biblical message is that of a *kerygma* and its interpretation is a task for the church, whereby the *kerygma* is set free and made accessible to understanding. This task needs sound guiding principles. In this sense the *meditatio* is a question of working out hermeneutical principles which shall have regard to the two conditions essential to any genuine interpretation: responsibility towards the text, and responsibility towards those for whom the interpretation is being provided.[19]

The above accounts of the hermeneutical principles are illustrated below:

BULTMANN'S HERMENEUTICAL METHOD

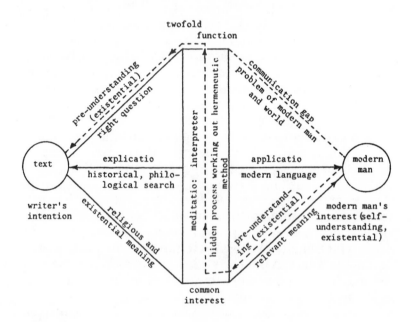

Diagram 2

In the above paragraphs and diagram, we have given only the merest outline of Bultmann's hermeneutical methodology, but insofar as our present thesis is concerned, enough has been said to make clear what principles his demythologizing is based on.

C.   Criticism of the Existential Interpretation

Now we are in a position to turn to some critics of Bultmann's existential interpretation. First of all, Karl Barth's and Karl Jaspers' criticisms are noteworthy and interesting for our hermeneutic point of view. The position of Barth and his followers is commonly known as right wing or orthodoxy, and Jaspers' and Fritz Buri's position as left wing. Barth's main criticism, broadly speaking, is that Bultmann identifies Christian existence with 'truly natural' existence. He does not think that natural self-understanding can serve as an introduction to the Biblical revelation.   Accordingly, Barth is very critical of Bultmann's hermeneutic method, that is, the existential question and the prior understanding existentially presupposed.

The critics of the other side, Jaspers and Fritz Buri, accuse Bultmann of not going far enough in his demythologizing.   Their existentialist position demands the removal of the *kerygma*, the proclamation of the act of God in Jesus Christ, which seems to them an inconsistent leap in Bultmann's existential interpretation.   Professor Macquarrie indicates that "they wish to remove the limit which Bultmann himself has set, and to merge theology into a philosophy of existence."[20]

In brief, Barth's criticism is of the method of Bultmann's *demythologizing* in order to rescue the *kerygma*, and Jaspers' and Buri's is the attack against the *kerygma* in order to seek a more liberal type of Christian interpretation. These two opposite positions of criticism have respectively their own weak points.   Barth who puts emphasis on God of *Totaliter aliter* and the vertical dimension of revelation has a problem in the area of intelligible communication because the *kerygma* must be a proclamation addressed to man who exists, and it must be unfolded in its existential significance.   On the other hand, the religious philosophy of Jaspers and Buri does not understand fully the meaning of the theological paradox in which the *kerygma*, the key message of God's redemptive act in Jesus Christ is indispensable in Christian faith.

Insofar as the context of the so-called right and left wing criticism is concerned, Bultmann's position seems to be regarded as a moderate and legitimate one because of his positive concerns and responsibilities both for *kerygma* and for modern intelligible communication. Yet those critics of the right and left sides also have value because Bultmann's *demythologizing* is in danger of becoming existentialist philosophy or anthropology on one hand, and of becoming involved in an abrupt and incongruous paradox which misleads Bultmann on the other. The criticisms from the both sides mean that Bultmann's *demythologizing* has a limit in its hermeneutic method.

However, the real serious criticism comes from another dimension of hermeneutics, linguistic philosophy, particularly the logical empiricists who have directed their attention to religious language. Dr. R.W. Hepburn, a linguistic philosopher, indicates that Bultmann's definition of myth is very ambiguous. It is too wide in its scope so as to include all pictorial, analogical and symbolical speech.[21]

In fact, Bultmann does not show any clear understanding of linguistic analysis and as Professor Macquarrie indicates, he "does not even betray any awareness of it."[22] As we know, Bultmann's *demythologizing* is to elucidate the meaning of Christian language, yet this hermeneutic intention is overwhelmed by his anthropological or existential terms. His further crucial mistakes come from the lack of knowledge of linguistic symbolism. Here is the point at which our main concern, the question of the spatio-temporal language comes in.

As we already mentioned, Bultmann's attitude to spatio-temporal language is almost negative as it objectifies non-objective reality. For him, the expressions like 'God is in heaven,' 'Christ descended into hell,' 'He will come as last Judge' are antiquated language incredible to modern man. According to Bultmann, all these statements are the misrepresentation of transcendental reality, and the objectification of the non-objective reality.[23]

In spite of his exclusive non-objective, existentialist interpretation, Bultmann admits in a later essay the inevitability of analogical language even though he uses the word without clear understanding. He says that "when we speak of an act of God, this is not pictorial but analogical language in which we represent God's act as analogy to a human act."[24] Professor Macquarrie points out, "the very fact that he uses the word, 'represent' (*vorstellen*), indicates that we have not entirely got away from images and pictures."[25] Nevertheless, Bultmann says that "to speak of God as acting is not to speak in symbols or images, but to speak analogically."[26] This confused statement is the evidence that Bultmann misunderstands the meaning of images, symbols and even analogy itself. Analogy is not separable from its symbolic function. Linguistic philosopher, Wilbur Urban's words make this relationship clearer. He says that "analogical predication is the very essence of the symbolic function."[27]

Here the concept of Bultmann's myth should be re-examined. He thinks that the images or symbols belong to a mythological category. This is another mistake. Again, Urban's words are noteworthy. "Myth is indispensable for the reason that it is only from the language of myth that the symbols of religion can be formed and only in such language that its real insights can be expressed."[28] Now we can understand the character of the spatio-temporal language of the New Testament. The language of space and time in religious faith is a highly symbolized and qualitative language which cannot be reduced to a scientific notion. Edwyn Bevan says that "the word for 'Height' is clearly used to signify what is sublime, wonderful, worthy of admiration."[29] Again, he says that "To call God the most high means that this value belongs to God in a supreme degree."[30]

Bultmann misses this dimension of the symbolic language because of his overemphasized existential concern. His anthropological and existential signification has an insight into 'deep content' which myth enshrines, yet he does not realize that the existential content is abstracted without its appropriate form. This kind of abstract content can be understood by intellectually trained people, but not by majority of people who prefer to feel and think in their ordinary and living language. In Bultmann's existential interpretation of the spatio-temporal language, there is, no doubt, a big gap between the content and form, in other words, reality and symbolic language.

The same can be said of the semantic problem, that is, meaning and linguistic form. Here it is worthy to quote Professor John MacMurray's words: "Where the logical empiricists discard the problems in order to retain the method, the existentialists relinquish the method in wrestling with the problems."[31] So the latter achieves a minimum of form, the former a minimum of substance. However, the above statement is right only when the empiricists discard the existential meaning of symbolic language. Adequate interpretation of symbolic language is to apprehend its inner reality. The form or expression is intrinsically related to its essence or reality. Especially religious forms including mythological language are more true in terms of their organic or wholistic unity and their symbolic meanings.

Nevertheless, Bultmann attempts to separate the content from its symbolic form. He emphasizes the existential meaning of the term 'here and now' as the content, and this brings a kind of a 'despatialization' and 'detemporalization,' which linguistic philosophers find in the law of development of language.[32] But his sharp contrast of the term with the imagery 'there and then,' which for Bultmann, would be taken as an objective language, shows no interest in cosmological and ontological dimension of spatio-temporal symbolism. Perhaps, it is for this reason that, in Bultmann's theology, there is little discussion about a cosmological and a futuristic dimension of hope.

Chapter III

Symbolic Interpretation and Space
and Time Language

Before discussing this subject, a few words about the title 'symbolic interpretation' should be said. We do not use the title to suggest that there is any symbolic school, as seen in the group of existentialist scholars, because actually there is no symbolic school and the title is not a product of any scholarly group. Nevertheless, there is a general agreement among scholars who are mostly critics of Bultmann's 'demythologizing' program. They attempt to emphasize the symbolic character of New Testament mythological language; in other words, their attempts are to give positive significance to that mythological language.

What, then, is the positive content? In order to answer this question, it is necessary to quote Giovanni Miegge. He writes, "The majority of these critics (of Bultmann) take refuge in that idea of myth which we have seen to be derived from the Platonic tradition."[1] It is true, they maintain, that myths are found in the New Testament; but, myth is the natural form for expression of religious experience and perhaps no substitute can be found for it. According to those critics, it is only through myth that the paradoxical event of Christ can be described. It cannot in any way be reduced to the categories either of rational or of historical thought -- the incursion of the transcendent, of 'the Word made flesh', into our history.

The idea of the symbolic character of the New Testament mythology is expressed by the New Testament scholars like Amos N. Wilder and Sherman Johnson. They assert that myth is an indispensable vehicle of religious truth, without which all religions, including the Christian gospel, would be condemned to silence. Mythological language is not an accurate, scientific description, but is allusive, poetic and imaginative. Sherman Johnson and Amos Wilder emphasize that the mythological language is symbolic, and suggestive of truth, viz., of transcendental truth, which cannot be conveyed by the use of ordinary descriptive, objectifying language. According to them, truth of this order cannot be communicated by any other language, e.g., by the discursive language of science.[2]

Burton H. Throckmorton's statement also is noteworthy on this question. He raises questions about Bultmann's non-mythological language, or existential language, and says, "I believe the answer to these questions must be 'No', for it appears that, aside from the question of whether or not New Testament mythology is true, the basic claim of the New Testament that in Christ all men may be saved, cannot be stated except in the language of myth."[3] When Throckmorton speaks about the mythological language, he refers emphatically to the universal significance of Christ's revelation. Thus he believes that myth is the only language in which such a vision, which sees heaven and earth, the beginning and the end all at once, can be expressed, for these are not seen upon scientific investigation, but only upon an encounter, at a profound level of experience, with the vicissitudes of life. He says,"It is through this encounter that God appears. Such an integrating vision requires its own means of expression, quite different from the language that describes specific observation; and this medium is myth."[4]

We could deal with more comprehensive discussions about myth here, but such matters are beyond the horizon

of this thesis.[5]   Rather we will turn to the relation of
mythology to image or symbolism. It is undoubted that
mythology and symbolism are inseparably related.
Following Ernst Cassirer's theory, John McKenzie identifies myth with symbolic expression. He writes, "the
writers of myth do not pretend to attain and describe as
immediately perceived in its concrete existence the reality with which the myth is concerned. They intend to present the reality in a symbolic form."[6] Here one important
point must be indicated: the distinction between myth and
symbolism. E. Cassirer says, "Mythical consciousness
lives in the immediate impression, which it accepts
without measuring it by something else. ... It is simply
overpowered by the object."[7]   In this sense mythical
language is characterized by intensity and immediate
power, and symbolic language is to be understood as much
more sophisticated with some understanding of the com-
plexity of its own logic. The very fact that we have words
like 'myth' and 'symbol' at all proves that we have emerged from a strictly mythical mentality. For this reason,
Professor Macquarrie makes a distinction between symbol and myth in terms of 'literal and critical stages' or 'un-
broken and broken myths' or 'dreaming and awake.'[8]
    Now let us consider the general meaning of sym-
bolism, particularly of religious symbol.

A.   General Views of Religious Symbolism

    As we know, many traditional symbols today have lost
their power. Yet with this, there has come an equally firm
conviction that man cannot live without symbols. What,
then, are the symbols to which our human life is ever
related? Here are some distinguished modern religious
thinkers whose studies on symbolism or symbolic models
are well known, starting with Edwyn Bevan's definition of
symbolism. While quoting A. N. Whitehead's words: "The
human mind is functioning symbolically when some components of its experience elicit consciousness, belief, emo-

tions, and usages, respecting other components of its experience," Edwyn Bevan defines the meaning of symbolism for his own purpose as the following. "A symbol certainly, I think, means something presented to the senses or the imagination usually to the senses which stands for something else. Symbolism in that way runs through the whole of life."[9]

Ernst Cassirer who built up his magisterial philosophy of *Symbolic Forms* "links together myth and religion and regards them both as the outward expression or manifestation of man's total feeling toward life."[10] This view is further developed by Susanne K. Langer, who acknowledges her deep indebtedness to Cassirer. She "regards myth and ritual as spontaneous expressions by which man transforms the emotions which naturally arise in his heart as he relates himself to life around him."[11] F. W. Dillistone, the editor of *Myth and Symbol*, says that in Cassirer's and S. Langer's view, "all symbolic forms whose primary reference is to the integration and renewal of the life of the universe may be regarded as essentially religious symbols."[12]

We will turn to another modern religious thinker and theologian, Paul Tillich, who has paid most attention to the place of symbols in the life of religion, and I will devote a good deal of space to dealing with his symbolism and symbolic interpretation, particularly of time and space language.

B.   Paul Tillich's Symbolism and Symbolic
      Interpretation

Paul Tillich declares,
Religious symbols.....are a representation of that which is unconditionally beyond the conceptual sphere; they point to the ultimate reality implied in the religious act, to what concerns us ultimately. ...
Religious symbols must express an object that by its very nature transcends everything in the world that is

split into subjectivity and objectivity.[13]

One of the reasons put forward by Tillich for the value of symbols is that there is a sickness and confusion of modern consciousness stemming from the decay of once vital images and symbols. Tillich here follows conclusions drawn from the psychology of C. G. Jung in which "certain archetypal symbols are universally present in the human-subconscious."[14] Jung predicts that the neglect of symbols and their loss of power result in paralysis and breakdown. He explains that symbols are vital for the necessary interplay of conscious and unconscious. Tillich understands a sacrament in this sense. He says that a sacrament "grasps our unconscious as well as our conscious being. It grasps the creative ground of our being."[15] This has a special point within the particular framework of Tillich's own system, for the unconscious is said to point to God, who is the ground of our being.

Another reason behind Tillich's preoccupation with symbols is his belief that a symbol differs from a sign because a symbol "participates in the reality of that for which it stands while the sign bears no necessary relation to that to which it points."[16] Here Tillich tries to emphasize the meaning of true religious symbols as participating in the power of the divine to which they point. However, he also says that religious symbols are double edged because they are directed not only toward the divine infinite, which they symbolize, but also toward the finite reality through which the divine referent is symbolized. Tillich believes that religious symbols "force the infinite down to finitude and the finite up to infinity. They open the divine for the human and human for the divine."[17] For instance, if God is symbolized as 'Father', he is brought down to the human relationship of father and child. But at the same time this human relationship is consecrated into a pattern of the divine-human relationship.

The above paragraphs are a brief introduction to Paul Tillich's theory of religious symbolism. To this, we can add his idea of symbolic interpretation. He puts an emphasis on the need of symbolic interpretation of religious language which enhances its reality and power. What does he mean by the symbolic interpretation? This question can be answered when we know Tillich's interest in theological movements such as Protestant Hegelianism and Catholic Modernism, which have interpreted religious language symbolically in order to dissolve its realistic meaning and to weaken its seriousness, its power, and its spiritual impact. For Tillich, the purpose and meaning of the symbolic interpretation is to give to God, and to all his relations to man, more reality and power than a non-symbolic, and therefore easily superstitious, interpretation could give them.[18]

One example of his symbolic interpretation can help our understanding. Tillich interprets, 'God as living' as a symbolic expression which participates in the reality it symbolizes. He says, "God lives in so far as he is the ground of life. Anthropomorphic symbols are adequate for speaking of God religiously."[19] Tillich stresses that the work of theology is to analyze the concrete symbols of the Bible, and interpret them in abstract ontological terms. It seems to me that Tillich's emphasis on interpreting the concrete symbols in abstract ontological terms is not far from W. M. Urban's metaphysical content of religious language. He says that, while the symbolic language of religious consciousness cannot abandon its concrete terms, so rich in colour, what it really means can be expressed only in terms of greater generality and abstractness.[20]

However, there is some vagueness and weakness in Tillich's approach to symbolism and symbolic interpretation. Now we are in a position to comment critically on Tillich's symbolism and symbolic interpretation. A. C. Thiselton says, "Symbols and symbolic language are powerful and perform valuable functions in calling forth engagement and response on the part of the hearer as well as in serving any more descriptive purpose that they can also achieve. Nevertheless, they also suffer from fundamental limitation, and cannot serve as adequate substitutes for cognitive discourse."[21] We acknowledge the power of symbol as grounded in our individual or collective unconsciousness. Yet this should not mean that the power of symbols says anything about their truth, because patients of certain mental illnesses may see an added symbolic significance in anything or everything.[22] Tillich does not pay enough attention to this problem.

The second criticism of Tillich's symbols is related to his assertion that a symbol 'participates' in that to which it points. According to Anders Jeffner, this idea is so ambiguous and ill-defined that its meaning is not clear at all.[23] Professor Macquarrie also acknowledges this ambiguity, yet tries to understand the word 'participation' as some intrinsic likeness between the analogue and that for which it stands. He says, "Perhaps the participation of an individual in a community gives us the best idea of what Tillich meant. For the individual and his community share certain basic human characteristics."[24] However, Tillich's word, 'participation' is still not clear to many other theological students, particularly when we ask about the participation of beings in Being which is basic to Tillich's theory of symbols.

Thirdly, there are questions about language use. Thiselton says, "it may seem as if 'white', for example, is necessarily symbolic of purity, or goodness. But in practice its use is culturally conditioned."[25] This means that symbols function with proper effect only when their use, or meaning is explained or interpreted in its context.

A fourth problem is that symbols do not describe or report historical states of affairs. This means that symbols include an element of timeless truth, but the Christian Gospel stresses God's unique act of salvation enacted at particular times and in particular places.

All this implies that "linguistic symbols perform valuable and indispensable functions, yet that they should be regarded as supplementary tools of language alongside other uses."[26] This means that we still need cognitive discursive language for adequate interpretation of the Christian message.

With the preceding account of general ideas about symbolism in mind, we can consider the symbolic interpretation of space and time language.   Here again, Tillich's interpretation will be introduced.   He deals with time and then space, and interprets time and space langauge in terms of categories of finitude which reveal their ontological character through their double relation to being and nonbeing.[27]   Tillich deals with four main categories in which the mind grasps and shapes reality: time, space, causality, substance.

For Tillich, the central category of finitude is time. He believes that time has both the positive and negative character, and that time moves from a past that is no more toward a future that is not yet through a present which is nothing more than the moving boundary line between past and future. For Tillich, time also has a creative character, and a directness and irreversibility, and a newness produced within it. This means that time, as experienced in immediate self-awareness, unites the anxiety of transitoriness with the courage of a self-affirming present. For Tillich, the anxiety concerning temporal existence is of existential character. The anxiety permeates the whole of man's being; it shapes soul and body and determines spiritual life. It is rooted in the structure of being. "Man would resign from having a present. Yet man affirms the present moment, though analytically it seems unreal, and he defends it against the anxiety its transitoriness created in him.   He affirms the present through an ontological courage which is as genuine as his anxiety about the time process."[28]

An interesting point Tillich makes here is to connect time with space through the meaning of the 'present'. He says, "The present always involves man's presence in it, and presence means having something present to one's self over against one's self (in German, *gegenwaertig*). The present implies space.   Time creates the present through its union with space. In this union time comes to a standstill because there is something on which to stand."[29]

This statement seems very interesting, yet it is ambiguous and speculative. Tillich, who stresses the need for symbolic interpretation of religious language, does not show enough knowledge of linguistic symbolism. The analytical study of human language tells us that the words or language are primarily spatial in character.

Bergson and thinkers following him have maintained that all our words for time had formerly a spatial meaning and that the vulgar notion of time is simply a copy of the notion of space. Urban believes that our intellect is primarily fitted to deal with space and moves most easily in this medium. Thus language itself becomes spatialized, and in so far as reality is represented by language, reality tends to be spatialized.[30] The adequate interpretation of the space-time language is to despatialize and detemporalize it.

But Paul Tillich tries to interpret the spatio-temporal language in terms of temporal primacy category which often seems to be an existential concept. We think that this is one of the reasons for the vagueness in his symbolic interpretation. His weak point is also found in the often quoted passage of his writing: "The statement that God is Being-itself is a non-symbolic statement. It does not point beyond itself. It means what it says directly and properly; if we speak of the actuality of God, we first assert that he is not God if he is not Being-itself. Other assertions about God can be made theologically only on this basis."[31] Later Tillich changed this statement and declared that the only non-symbolic assertion we can make about God is "the statement that everything we say about God is symbolic."[32]

Professor Macquarrie indicates that Tillich's initial attempt to explicate the use of 'Being-language' in respect of God was confused and this confusion was compounded through his use of such ambiguous expressions as 'ground of being,' 'power of being' and the like. Nevertheless, Tillich's theological insight into the role of space and time language is essentially correct.[33]

Here we have an example of his theological interpretation of the spatio-temporal language. The example starts with the interpretation of eternity. He uses our faith term, 'Eternity' as a symbol for all-temporality, and 'Omnipresence' as the spatial symbol.

What, then, does his concept of Eternity mean? It is the divine power which gives the courage to endure the anxiety of temporal existence. For Tillich, Eternal God means participation in that which conquers the nonbeing of temporality. He warns us against two misinterpretations of the concept of eternity:

> Eternity is neither timelessness nor the endlessness of time. The meaning of *olim* in Hebrew and of *aiones* in Greek does not indicate timelessness; rather it means the power of embracing all periods of time. Since time is created in the ground of the divine life, God is essentially related to it.[34]

Another misinterpretation is that eternity is the endlessness of time. "Endless time, correctly called 'bad infinity' by Hegel, is the endless reiteration of temporality.

To elevate the dissected moments of time to infinite significance by demanding their endless reduplication is idolatry in the most refined sense."[35]

On the basis of these considerations and the assertion that eternity includes temporality, Tillich interprets the relation of eternity to the modes of time in his analogical language by which he means a symbolic approach. He believes that the only analogy to eternity is found in human experience, that is, the unity of remembered past and anticipated future in an experienced present. Here his favourite phrase, 'an eternal present' (*nunc eternum*) is introduced as a symbolism. Tillich stresses the dominant character of the present in temporal experience. But his eternal present (*nunc eternum*) is not simultaneity or the negation of an independent meaning of past and future. "The eternal present is moving from past to future but without ceasing to be present. The future is genuine only if it is open, if the new can happen and if it can be anticipated."[36]

Tillich emphasizes the meaning of openness to the future as the characteristic of eternity. Yet this does not mean that he follows Bergson's idea of the absolute openness of the future which devaluates the present by denying the possibility of its anticipation. Tillich's future includes both elements, that is, openness for creativity on the one hand and limiting openness on the other. For him, to limit openness means the element in which the direction of history would be anticipated. Tillich's interpretation of the future in the light of God's eternity is connected with the meaning of the past. For him, God's eternity is not dependent on the completed past. He believes that for God the past is not complete, because through it he creates the future, and in creating the future, he re-creates the past. But the past includes its own potentialities. The past becomes something different through everything new which happens. The new aspect of the past becomes the basis for the historical interpretation of the past. In this sense Tillich believes that, from the point of view of eternity, both past and future are open. "The creativity which leads into the future also transforms the past. If eternity is conceived in terms of creativity, the eternal includes past and future without absorbing their special character as modes of time."[37]

In conclusion, we would say that Tillich's eternity is expressed in his temporal language which is interpreted in his ontological faith. This faith is the basis for a courage which conquers the negativities of the temporal process, and in which neither the anxiety of the past nor that of the future remains. Tillich declares that the anxiety of the past is conquered by the freedom of God toward the past and its potentialities. The anxiety of the future is conquered by the dependence of the new on the unity of the divine life. The dissected moments of time are united in eternity.[38]

Now we turn to Tillich's spatial language and his interpretation of it. As mentioned above, his symbolic term with respect to space is Omnipresence. God has relation to space, as his relation to time. God is neither endlessly extended in space nor limited to a definite space; nor is he spaceless. Tillich interprets the meaning of omnipresence in qualitative terms. He rejects pantheist formulation which interprets omnipresence as an extension of the divine substance through all spaces, because this subjects God to dissected spatiality and puts him, so to speak, alongside himself sacrificing the personal center of the divine life. Tillich also criticizes the attempt to interpret omnipresence to mean that God is present 'personally' in a circumscribed place (in heaven above) but also simultaneously present with his power every place (in the earth beneath). This is the criticism of the literal understanding of a tripartite view of cosmic space in terms of earth, heaven and underworld. Insofar as the criticism of the literal understanding of the three storied universe is concerned, Tillich's position is the same as that of Bultmann. Yet Tillich's view of spatial language as symbolic is different from that of Bultmann who rejects such spatial terms as an objectified, obsolete language. Tillich declares that theology must emphasize the symbolic character of spatial symbols, in spite of their rather literal use in the Bible and cult. Almost every Christian doctrine has been shaped by these symbols and needs reformulation in the light of a spatially monistic universe. "God is in heaven" means that God's life is qualitatively different from creaturely existence. But it does not mean that he 'lives in' or 'descend from' a spatial place.[39]

Finally, Tillich argues against the idea of omnipresence as spacelessness. Such idea is based, we are told, on an improper ontology, which affirms that extension characterizes bodily existence, which cannot be asserted of spiritual God, even symbolically. Tillich believes that God as Spirit includes the ontological element of vitality and personality which has a bodily basis. On this basis, he affirms the eternal presence of God and interprets the word *presence* to mean the combination of time and space.[40]

As we already mentioned, this interpretation is interesting, yet abstract and speculative. We wonder how such an interpretation can be understood as symbolic. It seems to us that he prefers an ontological philosophy to a symbolic, theological position. Tillich emphasizes the importance of symbolic interpretation of religious language, yet his method of interpretation lacks an analytical basis for empirical language. This is one of the main weak points that symbolic interpreters usually make. They demand symbolic interpretation of religious language, but they do not have a full knowledge of analytical and empirical language.

We have surveyed general ideas about symbolism and symbolic interpretation of religious language, and particularly examined Paul Tillich's symbolism and symbolic interpretation. With this account of the general views in mind, we can consider the symbols of the New Testament and its space and time relations.

C.   Some New Testament Scholars' Symbolic Interpretation of Space and Time Language

First of all, the question of whether Biblical language is symbolic or not is unavoidable. If it is symbolic, how symbolic is it? There is no doubt that, generally speaking, biblical mythology, especially the New Testament mythological language has symbolic character. People of Biblical lands and times expressed their religious beliefs and life by symbolic language. In the Bible there are innumerable symbolic words, phrases and stories: the light, darkness, wind, the tree of life and paradise story, etc.; these are only a few examples among many others. As A. Farrer, L. S. Thornton and T. Fawcett have reminded us,[41] the biblical writers make full use of this kind of symbolism. According to Giovanni Miegge,[42] even Bultmann shows stage-by-stage, with profound erudition and a deep religious sensitivity, that the mythological elements to be found in the writings of the New Testament are not actually mythological. He shows that they do not intend to be so, at least in the strict sense of the term; they are, more than anything else, a means of expression. They are symbols which bear relation to an object which in itself is not mythological, and to a profound spiritual experience out of which has arisen a new understanding of life, of man, above all of the self.

Let us, then, consider something of a few New Testament scholars' symbolic interpretation of space-time language. It is a great surprise to see that many critics of Bultmann's *demythologizing*, while they say much about symbolic language or the language of imagery, do not enter fully into a discussion of the significance of space-time relations. For instance, Amos Wilder and Sherman Johnson, in spite of their detailed discussions of Bultmann's *demythologizing*, do not show any interest in this problem. This is a weakness. Their concern is too much with the defense of outer form, that is to say, the 'shell' or 'husk' in which divine reality is contained, whereas the existentialists are too concerned with the existential *content* of myth. The exponents of symbolic interpretation are likewise too concerned with the symbolic form (or expression). Of course each of these must keep its balance, but more important is the problem of their organic unity. We think the problem cannot be solved until the matter of linguistic symbolism is seriously dealt with.

Although there is no full discussion of space and time language, however, some statements can be quoted from those who align themselves with symbolic interpretation of the New Testament mythology. Throckmorton says that "myth is the only language in which such a vision, which sees heaven and earth, the beginning and the end, all at once, can be expressed."[43] He puts emphasis on the inevitability of spatial language in the New Testament, interpreting thus:

> Heaven should be understood as where God is and we
> are not. Of course, as soon as one says 'where' he uses
> a word connoting a place in space; but spatial
> language is unavoidable because we have no other.
> Heaven means that God is above and must come to

us, for we can but try to reach him; He is raised and exalted, and we cannot reach him; for God will indeed not 'dwell on the earth' (I Kings 8:27). Heaven, then, cannot be thought of as a creation or created place, but only as 'where God is.' It is not created any more than God Himself is created. To be 'in heaven' is to be where God is rather than separated from Him -- to be reconciled to the Creator. Hell is, conversely, where God is not. Whether conceived of as the place where the dead are, or as the place of punishment, its meaning is that there man is separated from God and therefore cannot live. Like heaven, it ought not to be thought of as a created place, but as a mythological representation of the state of separation from the source of life.   Heaven and hell, then,   are mythological representations of meta-historical existence, either with or without God. Or, to put it another way, they represent life and death, reconciliation and estrangement, in historical existence.[44]

In the above quotation, we have an example of symbolic interpretation of New Testament spatio-temporal language, which is obviously different from existentialist interpretation, particularly regarding language of space and time.

Finally, we will add one more statement referring to space and time relations. Feine Behm Kuemmel says that they would limit the definition of myth to include only deeds of a divine being in time and space that have definite meaning for man's existence.[45]

As we have already suggested, the main concern of symbolic interpretation is to emphasize the symbolic form of space-time language, and actually the symbolic interpretation contributes to preserving mystery in the symbolic language. Nevertheless, the symbolic interpreters' language remains unconceptualized and does not show any definite meaning. Here then we introduce a third method of interpretation.

Chapter IV

Linguistic Symbolism and Space
and Time Language

In order to understand this third method, we may need
to reiterate the problem of the first two methods of interpretation. As we have seen, existential interpretation consists mainly of explicating the New Testament mythology
as a self-understanding, and of elucidating the existential
content in non-objectifying terms; in fact, this talk is intelligible when compared with a recognizable logic. Nevertheless, the existentialist language has a tendency to fly
off to a realm of pure speculation, and this is conspicuous
when we see the works of some German scholars like Ernst Fuchs and Gerhard Ebelling, who are still in
Bultmann's tradition.[1] It seems to be very doubtful how
much their discussion of *Sprachereignis* or *Wor-
tgeschehen* can be operative as communicating language
today. For this reason, the need for empirical language in
their discussion is inevitable, in addition to the matter of
outer form.

The problem is equally important for symbolic interpretation. In this case, the problem is to discover more
cognitive language for the explication of symbolic reality.
Symbolic interpretation is right in asserting symbolic
reality and its evocative, mysterious dimension, but it has
the tendency to lapse into obscurity and to perform its

function without conceptual elucidation of a symbol's meaning. This problem is also true of Paul Tillich's symbolic interpretation, which tries to seek an existential ontological relevance. For this reason, symbolic interpretation also requires empirical language which deals with a logical analysis of language.

A.   Language of Logical Empiricism
What, then, is the language of logical empiricism? Here we need a brief discussion of the contemporary linguistic philosophy, especially about the language of logical empiricism. As fully treated in Chapters 5 and 11 of his *God Talk* Professor Macquarrie discusses the earlier stage and later development of the new philosophical movement which has come to occupy so dominant a place in contemporary thought, especially in English-speaking countries. He describes that the main influences of the early stage are Ludwig Wittgenstein's *Tractus Logico-Philosophicus* and Alfred J. Ayer's *Language, Truth and Logic*, both of which are marked by logical analysis, linguistic interest and an empiricism. Yet both have positivistic views. According to these views, the only kind of meaningful language is the language which is made up of empirically verifiable assertions, and all other kinds of language are lumped together as 'emotive utterance.' Accordingly, such biblical or faith language as 'God is in heaven' is regarded as meaningless assertion because we cannot verify it by any relevant sense-experience.

However, logical positivism came to be less popular later, and a new movement which recognized a multiplicity of languages has developed. L. Wittgenstein, the author of the *Tractatus, Logico-Philosophicus* himself later recognized the multiplicity of 'language games' which stresses, among other things, that language represents an activity of life, and may therefore take as many forms as life itself: giving orders, describing an object's appearance, reporting an event, making up a story, guessing riddles, telling a joke, asking, thanking, cursing, greeting, praying.[2] 'Commanding, questioning, recounting, and chatting are as much as a part of our natural history as walking, eating, drinking, or playing.[3] This means that words have meaning only in the stream of thought and life. Following this later Wittgenstein, modern linguistic analysts tell us that the meaning of language is to be sought in the way it gets used. Every language has its logic. This means that religious language also has its logic which is used by the religious believer. Religious or theological language constantly employs ordinary words in special settings or contexts which decisively determine their meanings. The decisiveness of setting or context, as over against vocabulary, may be illustrated further both from theological and non-theological examples. Wittgenstein notes the way in which setting determines meaning in the case of the word 'exact.'[4] What does 'exact' mean? In the setting of astronomy the 'exact' distances between two stars would hardly be measured in inches. But in microbiology the 'exact' distance between two molecules would mean something very different.

A further set of examples can be found in the biblical language, especially in the Fourth Gospel. Understanding, in John, does not depend mainly on mere word-recognition. It may be part of the Johannine irony that on more than half a dozen occasions listeners mistake the meanings of ordinary familiar words because these words perform their functions in special context. In John 4:3-4, Nicodemus fails to understand the meaning of 'birth' until Jesus explains to him that 'water and the spirit' define the setting of the term and thus determine its meaning. Similarly in John 4:10-12, the woman of Samaria misunderstands the term 'living water,' and in the same chapter Jesus' disciples misunderstand the meaning of the every day word 'food': 'He said to them, "I have food to eat of which you do not know." So the disciples said to one another, "Has anyone brought him food?" Jesus said to them, "My food is to do the will of him who sent me."' (John 4:32-34). Large stretches of the sixth chapter turn on misunderstandings about such words as 'bread,' 'blood,' 'drink' and 'come down' because their Christological setting gives them a different meaning from that of their usual settings in every day life.[5]

B.   Existential and Ontological Meaning of Space and Time Language

In this connection, it would be worth noting the views of two other philosophers, W.M. Urban and Martin Heidegger. Although they approach language from very different directions, each in his own way stresses that the problem of communication cannot be solved in terms of the recognition of individual words or vocabulary alone. W. M. Urban, the author of *Language and Reality*, repeatedly stresses that language needs to be viewed within the living human context where alone it functions. His emphasis on semantic context shows that there are different levels of context, that is, the linguistic (or grammatical) context, vital context (or situation) and a still further widening context, the "Universe of Discourse"[6] which is Urban's new terminology. Urban acknowledges that in these contexts, even in the grammatical context, human intentionality is involved, and is the part of the context in which the meaning subsists. Here it is necessary to introduce Urban's law of language development, which comes from E. Cassirer's. According to this law, our human language moves or develops from the physical to the universal or spiritual, which means the upward movement of language. This is particularly true of space and time language. All words, Urban believes, have unquestionably an original physical reference,[7] and also words for *relations* are primarily spatial in character. For instance, the words like 'standing for' 'referring to' 'beyond our knowledge' have a primarily spatial meaning which is never completely lost. The outstanding case, Urban indicates, is the relation expressed by spatial words 'in' or 'within.' We know that the word 'in' has many different meanings like 'I live in Canada,' or 'That is in my power,' or 'We are all in Christ.'

The above statements show the process of despatializing the spatial language or of spiritualizing it.[8] Here we
can acknowledge that there is one important point to be
noted as to the personal dimension and creative element in
the development of language. Urban puts emphasis on this
element in his semantic discussion: "There is no semantic
meaning situation which does not involve as necessary
components both speaker and hearer."[9]
    Let us turn to M. Heidegger's view. He also stresses
the need to place language in context if its meaning is to be
properly grasped. He believes that any interpretation
depends on a whole unspoken background of knowledge
and experience.[10] His emphasis on the context involves the
existential meaning of the context. Here it is necessary to
see Heidegger's linguistic analysis, especially about a
philosophical phenomenon of the language of space and
time.   This analysis is examined by Professor
Macquarrie:

> He(**Heidegger**)fastens onto the fact that, according to
> some philologists, the preposition 'in,' which we nor-
> mally use to designate a spatial relation between en-
> tities, is derived from an old verb, *innan*, 'to dwell'. It
> is maintained that the preposition has been derived
> from the verb, and not vice versa. Now it is obvious
> that 'to dwell in' means very much more than merely
> 'to be located in'. Certainly, 'to dwell' includes the
> spatial relation, but it involves a host of other rela-
> tions besides -- what we may call existential relations,
> such as practical concern, familiarity, affection, and
> so on. (**Cf. the Latin verb** *colere*, **which means 'to**
> **dwell,' 'to cultivate,' 'to take care of,' 'to reverence'**).
> A process of abstraction has taken place in the mean-
> ing of the word 'in,' whereby the sense of spatial loca-
> tion has more or less displaced the other possible
> senses. But Heidegger does well to remind us of the
> existential matrix of meaning behind the word,
> especially as we may still hear someone saying that
> he is 'in' love, or a theologian declaring that God was
> 'in' Christ, where we would completely misunders-

tand what was meant if we thought that 'in' had a spatial sense."[11]

Heidegger's view of language might be incompatible with the law of development of language of which linguistic philosophers speak.[12] But as Professor Macquarrie says, "the question of whether his view is in conflict with the progressive view of language or not is not important here, insofar as his purpose in this analytical study of language is not to glorify primeval language.[13] More important is that Heidegger's existentialism is approached by linguistic analysis and that the former is getting close to linguistic symbolism.

The above paragraphs are the discussions about the need of semantic context and its internal meaning of personal or existential content. Now we have to go to another aspect of religious language, its ontological dimension. Urban sees the ontological reality of language when he says the cosmological propositions of religious language and its cosmic significance of values. He says, "The cosmological propositions are fundamentally of two kinds, assertions about the creation of the world and assertions about its end or destiny."[14] When the Christian creed asserts that God is the maker of heaven and earth and of all things visible and invisible, it implies something of tremendous significance although it is said symbolically. This is also true when a Last Judgement is expressed in the same creed. The notions like 'maker,' 'heaven,' 'last judgement' or 'first and last thing' are inseparable from the cosmological significance of space and time which is basal in every religious view of the world.

When we interpret cosmological language, the most important thing is to know what it really wants to say. Urban here mentions the cosmic significance of values. He believes that religious consciousness uses concrete cosmic terms, so rich in colour, which belong to its poetical and mythical aspects, yet what it really means can only be interpreted in terms of greater generality and abstractness, which means the cosmic significance of values. The cosmological language and its significance culminate in its ultimate value of God or absolute Being. The space and time language contains implicitly an assertion about the ultimate nature of reality, and about the fullness of being. Urban says that "The explicit statements of the space and time language are mythological in the neutral and technical use of the word myth, and symbolic in the sense that the things 'that are unseen' are expressed in the terms of the things that are seen," but what it really says, is its ultimate ontological content, which can be expressed only in the language in which "value and reality are inseparable.-- the identity of the *summum bonum* or *ens perfectissimum* with the *ens realissimum* ".[15]

As shown in the above discussions, insofar as the ultimate ontological reality of the religious language is concerned, Heidegger's view is not far from Urban's view although their approaches are not the same. In his late work, Heidegger comes near to a more explicit ontological position identifying Being and language. Professor Macquarrie quotes Heidegger's words, "The essence of language is the language of essence." By the essence of language, he means Being's self-expression to us in language.[16] In this statement, we can acknowledge that Heidegger's concern is not only with an existential phenomenon, but also with an ontological dimension of language. Macquarrie interprets Heidegger's concern in terms of 'existential-ontological' language. He also comments that the ontological aspect of Heidegger is not far from the biblical conception of revelation of God. He quotes a remark of Laszlo Versenyi: "The quasi-biblical tone of Heidegger's pronouncement is quite appropriate to what he is trying to say. For in his conception of thought — as thought by Being, for Being and of Being — the importance of the thinker as a self-certain subject is as much reduced as it is in the biblical conception of revelation of God, by God and for the greater glory of God. At the same time, just as in and through biblical revelation, man obtains a new dignity as the preserver of the truth."[17] The last part of the above quotation attracts our special attention because of its value relations. When 'the preservation of its truth' is mentioned, Heidegger's Being is close to Urban's belief in the conservation of value. Values not only have cosmic significance but also ontological significance.[18] Urban interprets the notion of the conservation of values in terms of the idea of time and temporal process, that is, time language, which is to be interpreted in terms of a timeless and metaphysical relation of 'good' or value to being.[19]

Finally to this ontological discussion of religious language, I would like to add another insight which Bishop Ian Ramsey's *Religious Language* deals with. Ian Ramsey, an analytic philosopher, has consistently tried to set religious language in religious situations, which he has very well characterized as a situation of 'discernment and commitment.' In making this double characterization, Ramsey acknowledges not only the personal and committal factor of religious language, but also its cognitive dimension which other analytic philosophers are reluctant to acknowledge. By the cognitive dimension of 'discernment' Ramsey means the discernment or disclosure of some trans-human reality, and this idea indicates that he is prepared to set this language ultimately in its ontological context.

In concluding this part of the thesis, we present the following diagram:

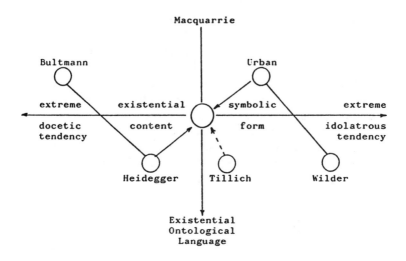

Diagram 3

The above diagram indicates several points:

(1) In the divided horizontal line, Heidegger and Bultmann are on the side of the existential dimension, while Urban and Wilder on the side of symbolic language. But Heidegger and Urban are closer than the two others through their linguistic approach, in which the existential and ontological dimension of patio-temporal language is discovered and interpreted.

(2) The two extreme positions on mythological language, that is, the existential interpretation and symbolical interpretation, can be resolved only when philosophical methods of linguistic analysis and interpretation are supplied from outside (non-theological).

(3)   The vertical line indicates that Macquarrie's language of existence and being is situated on the middle point between Heidegger and Urban.

(4) The broken, slanted line indicates Tillich's shaky and uncertain position. Tillich attempts to relate the two different points of existential and ontological interpretations, yet the bridge is slender, and his symbolic interpretation is not clear enough.

(5) The two dimensions, existential and symbolic, can be restated in terms of content and form, and when the two go to their respective extremity, they have the tendency to fall into docetism or idolatry.

C.   Dialectic of Semantic Form and Content

This last section of our methodological discussions will be devoted to constructing an adequate semantic rule or principle of religious language, especially of space and time language, then we may apply this semantic guidance to case studies while concluding the above hermeneutical approaches, that is the existential and symbolic interpretations.

As already indicated, the central problem of hermeneutical methodology is the separation or ambiguous relation between the semantic form and content. The problem of existential interpretation was the overemphasis on the existential depth content, that of the symbolic approach, the other extremity which stresses the symbolic form or expression. The result is that the former has a Gnostic or docetic tendency which an intellectual minority often falls into. The latter has an idolatrous inclination which often discards the conceptual articulation. For this reason, the linguistic approach of logical empiricism has been considered as a mediation or a bridge to solve the problem of the gap between form and content.

However, unless the nature and function of language is further clarified, the mediating approach of logical empiricism cannot lay claim to the final methodological answer. What, then, is language? This is the classical question which has a long history and raises modern epistemological disputes. This is not the place to survey the classical discussion, yet it is necessary to point out its key idea in our hermeneutical context.

Language can be understood in terms of the semantic form and content. This formula might seem at first sight to be too wide and ambiguous. However, examined closely, all our human life and linguistic existence are based on this dichotomous structure. The formula of form and content and vice versa can be reformulated or extended in more sophisticated terms and in different contexts: language and thought, expression and meaning, Kant's sensible intuition and concept, Noam Chomsky's surface structure and deep structure, Paul Ricoeur's logos and bios; or Gadamer's 'linguistic form and content' as hermeneutical experience. In spite of their different terms and different contexts, these insights into the abiding structure of reality or truth are not very different from each other. The ever-increasing sophistication of the dichotomy seems that our human existence is a permanent search or exploration for the mystery of our constituent structure, the body and spirit. The mysterious unity or tension of the visible and invisible, of expressible and inexpressible is an unceasing, ever-questionable dichotomy. The unity or tension of the two entities is not to be understood as a platonic or some other dualistic structure, but as a dialectic movement. Insofar as the dichotomy of the bodily system and spirit is concerned, it is clear that the former cannot be the permanent organic part of reality. We know that a spiritually keen patient who suffers from a deadly disease stands out of the boundary of his body system. The body form or visible organic system is subject to the destiny of spatio-temporal finitude.

Then how about the spiritual reality? Most religious languages do not accept that physical death is a termination of life. St. Paul says, "If our hope in Christ is good for this life only, and no more, then we deserve more pity than anyone else in all the world." (I Cor. 15:19) Does this, then, suggest that the invisible reality of spirit has supremacy over the bodily existence? The answer to this question is not easy without religious faith and language.

Let us then turn to our subject, the formula of the linguistic form and content. Philosopher Gadamer tries to understand the dichotomy in terms of hermeneutical experience when he says that "Linguistic form and content that has been handed down cannot be separated in hermeneutical experience."[20] For him, the hermeneutical experience involves the linguistic nature of the human experience of the world and its extended horizon. He says that "the linguistic world in which we live is not a barrier that prevents knowledge of being in itself, but fundamentally embraces everything in which our insight can be enlarged and deepened."[21]   In our context, Gadamer's linguistic form and content are an indissoluble unity of language and thought, yet, involves the hermeneutical phenomenon.

The intimate unity or the inseparability of language and thought has been the premise from which philosophy of language started. Linguistic philosophers have come to a general agreement with what word and thought, *sprache* and *geist* are inseparable. This means that "the problem of what we can know is so closely bound up with the question of what we can say, that all meditation on knowledge involves mediation on speech."[22]

However, the acknowledgement of the inseparability of the two entities is not enough to solve the semantic problem. The further question is how the two, that is, the form and content are related. In other words, what kind of relation exists between speech and thought. There has often been an idea of organic unity, so to speak, a psychosomatic kind of answer. Yet it seems to us that this answer is of a static or compromising kind. Language is a dynamic movement; its form and content have the character of mobility. The nature of language should be found in its upward movement from the physical through an analogical to symbolic reference. It moves "from what is known to what is yet to be known."[23] This means that the semantic form is not static and changeless.

The linguistic form, as the function of expression and communication, moves forever upward to follow the unexpressible spiritual meaning or experience. Our vocabulary, or words as signs, are not unlimited in number, yet our human linguistic function transforms the limited signs into unlimited, meaningful forms. In this process, there is an ever-increasing semantic detachment. For example, our experience of cold weather is primarily a physical one, yet its meaning does not remain static. The semantic meaning is detached from the primary perception and moves to an analogical or symbolical reference like 'coldness in reception' or 'cold war,' through various contextual changes or different literary forms. The idiomatic use of language, metaphor, allegory, analogy, symbolism or many other different literary forms are all modes of semantic detachment. In the case of religious language, especially spatio-temporal language, the detachment is further apparent.

Our human existence is conditioned by spatial and temporal finitude. Thus our human language, when examined closely, is basically of spatial and temporal character. This is particularly true of religious experience and language, which includes the words and stories about 'heaven,' 'hell,' 'ever-lasting God,' or 'eternal life.' The primary meaning of the space and time words is physical experience, yet its semantic meaning is detached from the original sense and moves to the spiritual reference through indirect language such as parables, metaphors, and various narrative forms.

However, for further understanding of the meaning of semantic detachment, two elements of linguistic function, an intrinsic or intuitive meaning and extrinsic meaning should be considered. The former belongs to a kind of connotative function of language, the latter denotative. The intrinsic or intuitive sense is that which "does conjure up and make us relive objects, situations, characters in a way quite different from the conceptual description of 'science.'"[24] I believe that this intrinsic or intuitive meaning is a basic content without which no semantic detach-

ment and movement can be made. To make the intrinsic
or intuitive meaning clearer, a quotation can be made
from Urban. He says, "When I am thirsty I pick up a glass
of water and drink it. When I am tired, seeing a chair, I sit
down. In each case the meaning is an *integral* part of the
datum: it is, so to speak, blended with it and is apparently
as much a part of it as any of the sense qualities...Mean-
ings, once assigned as intrinsic qualities of objects, are
then as immediately given in *intuition* as are sense
data."[25]   This intrinsic or intuitive content has the
character of a self-encircling connotation which does not
point beyond the datum of which it is the meaning.

Here another function of language, the extrinsic meaning comes in. The character of extrinsic meaning is that
the very essence of the meaning lies in this pointing or
reference. Again an illustration can help our understanding of extrinsic meaning: "Clouds mean rain, A grimace
means pain"[26] This kind of meaning is that in which one
perceptual object suggests or indicates another--is in fact
a sign of the other. We can call this transference the start
of semantic detachment. In this process or movement
their first or primary meaning of the word is transferred to
its analogical or symbolical meaning. In this detachment
here enters into the situation a certain individuation of
both the sign and the thing signified, a certain polarity of
indicator and indicated, which are not present on the level
of intrinsic meaning. For Urban, this point is that "interpretation -- or understanding -- of the sign *as sign* first
enters in. He says that 'until this element of polarity appears, 'meaning' means only a cue to adaptive movement or to emotive reaction."[27]

How can then the transference or detachment be
made? And what is the element of the transference or
detachment? Let us start with the second question. The
element or factor of the detachment is the meaning of the
language, not signs of things or happenings. Mt. Sinai
itself is just a fixed sign, yet the words 'Mt. Sinai' as expressive signs implies many significations. The element
of detachment or transference is the very meaning of the

word expression. In this sense, the meaning of these words is mobile. This character of mobility involves the universal and communicative function of language. The words 'Mt. Sinai' as expressive signs have a universal implication in which there is a mutual acknowledgment among the people all over the world.

Let us, then, turn to the first question, how can the transference or detachment be made? This question is related to the one just discussed. Yet the important thing is to acknowledge the dynamic aspect of communication in terms of "intentionality" of linguistic meaning. There is no doubt that the meaning of language implies the factor of intentionality. This intentionality presupposes the semantic meaning situation. The semantic meaning situation has not only two primary components, the sign and thing signified, that which means and that which is meant. But there also is a third factor, that is someone for whom it is a sign, someone for whom the meaning is. The other words, the completion of a semantic meaning situation requires the third component of a speaker or a hearer. There is no semantic meaning situation which does not involve as necessary components both speaker and hearer. Here the element of intentionality operates between the two through words as expressive signs. The words as such are characterized by intentionality, and this intentionality implies communication, either implicitly or explicitly.

In this connection, the etymological meaning of the word 'express' as 'ex-press' (pressare), which implies a dynamic sense of intentionality is of great significance. This also shows the contact point between language and its semantic meaning, in other words, between the linguistic form and content. Expression of language means not only its outward form, but also its inner content as intentional dynamism. In this sense, the dynamic meaning of Incarnated Logos as God's expression can be considered. The word as God's Logos is his powerful saving intention or will and also his linguistic sign which has the function of universal human communication. This means that language, in an ultimate and general sense, is not of a static kind, but is mobile and dynamic. What, then, is the need for mobility? Its movement involves a value dimension. The intentionality of the semantic meaning has its purpose and value dimension, which searches for its universal or ideal communication. Unless it is a corrupt or fallible language, any normal usage of a word has intentionality of ideal or universal value. When someone says, "He is a handsome person," the expression is not only descriptive language. It also expresses his personal quality. Of course there are many objective or descriptive types of language, including scientific and logical statements. However, even this kind of description, when examined closely, includes the element of value predication. The affirmation or negation of logical judgement itself belongs to a kind of value judgement. However, we are concerned with language in general, albeit particularly Christian, religious language. Christian biblical language, particularly the language of Incarnation, is value-oriented. It includes value words of light, glory, as well as spatio-temporal imageries. We will have further discussions about this subject later.

Now we turn to the linguistic form, or the outward aspect of language or discourse. Thus far we have considered mainly the semantic meaning or context of language. As we have stressed, our methodological concern in this study is to solve the problem of linguistic forms and content (meaning). The latter has been characterized by semantic mobility which cannot be separable from the outward form, the *ex-form* of *expression*. Here the meaning of 'outward' not 'outer' should be noted. The former suggests the inseparable relation to the pressure of intentional meaning while the word 'outer' may mean separability of the reality in terms of 'outer' and 'inner.'

Our contention as regards to the linguistic form or the outward form of language is that form also has a mobile character. As we mentioned earlier in this section, the linguistic form is to follow up the dynamic movement of the semantic content. This does not suggest any separability of the two entities because without the outward form or 'ex-form,' there is no possibility of knowing the semantic meaning or content. In fact, the outward form itself is a part of the whole semantic reality. Nevertheless, for our descriptive purpose, the division of the form and content is possible and necessary.

The form or outward form of language can be examined by Husserl's phenomenological term 'Gestalt.' He has examined the conditions of understanding speech, or of semantic meaning, and finds them to consist of the two factors, that is 'Gestalt' and 'intention.' However, here we are concerned with 'Gestalt' to explicate the structure of the form in our context. Here we will follow Urban's analysis of the 'Gestalt.' 'Gestalt' or the form, we are told, has two levels of structure, that is, surface level and internal level. On the surface, the distinction between meaningful and meaningless speech or sentences is the matter of a mere arrangement of pattern. For instance, a pseudo phrase such as "large brown on" does not have meaning even though the elements are recognized. Any meaningful structure implies a certain arrangement of form or pattern, not the meaningless combination of sounds or individual words. Understanding is then conditioned by apprehension of pattern (Gestalt). However, for genuine understanding of language, there must be what many linguists describe as "inner speech form." Von Humboldt introduced this notion to distinguish the unique character of a particular language from the element common to all languages.

The notion of 'the inner speech form' is of special importance in connection with the problem of translation. How can one language be translated to another language in spite of their spatially or temporally different context? The problem arises even within the same speech community. For example, the English word 'love' may have different meanings. For one, it may mean merely the biological urge and its consummation; for another, it may mean something quite different. Nevertheless, there is genuine communication and understanding by the reason of the mutual acknowledgement of the same universe of discourse and of its presuppositions. Here, Urban points out the importance of certain values. He says that what is presupposed is the mutual acknowledgement of certain values. This mutual acknowledgement of values conditions all intelligible communication--all meaning ultimately goes back to values.[28]

Now it is necessary to reassess the above "Gestalt" structure in the light of modern linguistic and hermeneutical research.

The "Gestalt" structure of the surface and inner form has a certain similarity with Noam Chomsky's "surface structure" and "deep structure." For Chomsky, the main concern is syntactic structure which describes the meaning structure of the semantics. As linguistic philosopher John Searle says, for Chomsky, "the heart of the grammar is the syntax."[29] His 'surface' and 'deep' structure is the result of the syntactical study. However, Chomsky's linguistic analysis gives us clearer knowledge about the semantic structure even though he does not use the term "Gestalt" or "the form." Chomsky's emphasis is on the "deep structure" while indicating ambiguous character of "surface structure." One simple illustration can help our understanding. The sentence "I like her cooking" is remarkably ambiguous. It can mean, among other things, I like what she cooks, I like the way she cooks, I like the fact that she cooks, even, I like the fact that she is being cooked. How can we account for these cases where one sentence containing unambiguous words has several different meanings? Chomsky claims that "these sentences have several different syntactical structure, that the uniform *surface* structure of, e.g., 'I like her cooking' conceals several different *underlying* structure which Chomsky called 'deep structure.'"[30]

However, Chomsky's syntactical conclusion has a problem in the semantic area. John Searle points out that the defect of the Chomskyan theory is "the failure to see the essential connection between language and communication, between meaning and speech acts. The picture that underlies the semantic theory, and indeed Chomsky's whole theory of language is that sentences are abstract objects that are produced and understood independently of their role in communication."[31]

Chomsky's problem is that he sees language as a self-contained formal system used more or less incidentally for communication. Searle suggests that the study of semantic competence should be approached from the point of view of the ability to use sentences to perform speech acts, and in this connection, the meaning of intentionality is emphasized. He says that "saying something and meaning it is essentially a matter of saying it with the intention to produce certain effect on the hearer. For example, the speaker who knows the meaning of the sentence 'The flower is red' knows that its utterance constitutes the making of a statement. But making a statement to the effect that 'The flower is red' consists in performing an actin with the intention of *producing in the hearer the belief* that the speaker is committed to the existence of a certain state of affairs, as determined by the semantic rules attaching to the sentence."[32]

Searle's view quoted above can be good ground for the subject "intention," which Husserl offers as another semantic factor. According to Husserl, there the understanding of semantic meaning involves more than the Gestalt structure in which the surface and inner speech form are included. The essence of semantic meaning, we are told, is its intentionality, and understanding of the meaning involves the apprehension and acknowledgement of this intentionality.

The emphasis on semantic intentionality demands further content of language, which includes the value dimension of language. Language gains its reality through communication that it comes into being, and this involves the universal value words of speech community. Human intentionality implies the historically transmitted value consciousness of community life. Of course, we do not deny that there is specific language which has no more or less relation with the value elements than purely mathematical or logical affirmations. However, as mentioned previously, such logical or descriptive language, strictly speaking, also includes certain value forms because judgement or logical affirmation is of a kind of value relation.

However, our concern here is not to prove the validation of the value category. It is sufficient to admit that our ordinary, and particularly religious talk is value-oriented language. One of the Far Eastern sayings goes that even a thief does not tell his own son to steal. Our historical human life is surrounded or conditioned by all kinds of value relations. This means that our human existence is inseparable from aesthetical or ethical reality, both individually and socially.

We think that the origin of value consciousness is from its negative reality. The appreciation of the beautiful or the good is based on its negative counterparts, the ugliness or the wrong, which reflect historical situations of human existence. Although the P Source of Genesis chapter one stresses the affirmative side of God's creation when it says, "And God saw that it was good," the reality of the value is better understood by the consciousness of the negative value, that is, guiltiness or darkness, which is presupposed in the affirmative language.

However, our concern here is not to establish any priority between the doctrine of original sin and that of original goodness, but to emphasize the reality of the value dimension which is intrinsically related to human life. The greater importance is that the value dimension is closely related to space and time language. This truth is first found in the Creation story of the first chapter of Genesis:

> And God said, 'Let there be lights in the firmament of the heavens to separate the day from the night; and let them be for signs and for seasons and days and years, and let them be lights in the firmament of the heavens to give light upon the earth. And it was so. And God made the two great lights, and greater light to rule the day, and the lesser light to rule the night; he made the stars also. And God set them in the firmament of the heavens to give light upon the earth to

rule over the day and over night, and to separate the light from the darkness. And God saw that it was good.' (Gen. 1;14-18)

The above biblical quotation shows how the space and time words are closely related to the highly symbolical or universal value words, such as light or darkness. These words are also related or extended to other quality language: graceful, holy, powerful, majestic, etc. W. Urban describes such adjectives as graceful, wild, etc., in terms of *"Gestalt-qualitat, "* 'form-quality,' which involves the notion of the experience of quality.

In this connection, something about adjectival semantics should be considered. The basic parts of language, the noun, the verb, and the adjective all require intuitive involvements. As Urban describes, the intuitive content or meaning of the noun is ideal unity or individuality and that of the verb is activity content. But more clearly, intuitive content or meaning is found in the adjective entity which is described as the *Erlebnisswert* of quality and values.[33] The recognition of this adjectival semantics is of special importance for religious language, most particularly in connection with our space and time semantics.

Nevertheless, many philosophical and theological studies of language lack this crucially important point in their discussions. For instance, Paul Ricoeur's basic structure of discourse semantics consists of "a noun and a verb which are connected in a synthesis which goes beyond the words."[34] Ricoeur stresses the status of the sentence as a single distinctive trait, which has a predicate. For him, the subject is the bearer of a singular identification and what the predicate says about the subject can always be treated as a "universal feature of the subject. Ricoeur's emphasis here is on the universal function of the predication, while the polarity and interplay between the singular identification of subject (noun) and the universal predication (verb) are recognized from the point of view of the propositional content. The importance of the predicate is found in designating 'a kind of quality, a class of things, a type of relation, or a type of action.'"[35]

Ricoeur's view is generally true, yet the range of the predicate is too wide and ambiguous to grasp. The reason for this is that he does not see another entity of semantic structure, that is the adjectival function. This function has its own right or status which should not be included in a lump under the category of predication. Especially when we deal with religious language the importance of the adjectival entity is clear. The semantics of religious language, particularly the space and time language emphatically includes the adjectival dimension and its intuitive meaning. As Urban writes, "the adjective, as the word indicates, is the speech form which *attaches* an quality to an object or entity, and to attach it presupposes that there has already been a detachment from the immediate living experience of the object."[36] In this sense, Urban describes poetic diction as having the power of conjuring up the living reality itself. For instance, "Red blooms the Rose," or "Wild blows the wind," are examples of poetic Gestalt or arrangement in which the poet detaches from the object a vital quality which is, so to speak, a part of its very life. This intuitive meaning of the "red" and the "wild" can be lived --*erlebt.* [37]

The above statements indicate the semantic ground of linguistic value dimension. To sum up, the semantic content of the language, particularly religious, has its intuitive ground before it is developed into conceptual words; and the intuitive content or semantic meaning is particularly clear when we examine the qualitative entity of the adjective, in which all different levels of value words are involved. This does not mean that the speech parts of noun and verb are of less importance. The noun and verb as the unit of propositional form cannot be separated from the adjective reality as its qualitative universal while all of the main speech parts include some different degrees of intuitive meaning.

Our emphasis on the adjective or qualitative entity is to rediscover the semantic ground of religious language in which various qualitative or value forms are involved. The value words like "high," "deep," "majestic," "powerful," "righteous," "merciful," and their opposites are all adjectival relations. We admit that poetic diction has intuitive power and quality in which aspects of lived experience are represented in appropriated image form. In a similar way, the semantic quality and value are experienced in religious language and life.

This value language is particularly important in the Christian Scripture. The Bible is abundant in such value words, especially together with spatial and temporal expressions. This spatial-temporal and value language finds its paramount expression in theophany language like "Shekhinah" in the Wilderness of the Exodus story, and in Christological stories, as Christ's pre-existence, Incarnation and Exaltation. Here spatio-temporal language is confessional faith language. A further point is that this spatio-temporal theophany or Christological language often accompanies the qualitative value words for its universal communication. The words such as holy, light, glory, or graceful are highly symbolized qualitative forms of language which have universal religious significance.

Now we will conclude this chapter with the following points. First of all, our semantic problem of space and time language is to be solved through an adjectival value dimension. The value consciousness and its direction or goal are detached from the present existence of worldliness and are to be transformed into trans-spatial and trans-temporal ultimate value reality. This meaning can be better understood by spatio-temporal imagery language, like the story of the ancient Hebrew's wandering about in the wilderness and marching to the Promised land, the Ascension story of Christ, and John Bunyan's *Pilgrim's Progress.* These stories of spatial image have more appealing power than any other stories. The Old Testament story of pilgrimage to the Promised land is of the more existential kind, and the Ascension of Christ is of cosmological significance in which God's redemptive work is shown as the victorious way to the heavenly home. New Testament Christology stresses Christs's saving act in terms of overcoming (Synoptic and Acts), or passing through (the Epistle to Hebrews) the spatio-temporal boundaries.

Firstly, we can re-affirm that the semantic meaning of language, particularly the semantics of New Testament space and time language has God's saving act as its semantic content: God's word and its historical predication; that is, "the Word became flesh and dwelt among us, full of grace and truth; we have beheld his glory, glory as of the only Son from the Father." (John 1:14) This incarnated Word implies that God's dynamic intention and loving action was shown in concrete space and time situation so that sinful and hopeless human beings can be delivered from their miserable dark situations. God's eternal and heavenly glory in the incarnated Christ is the inward meaning or content of the New Testament Christological language, which has the highest value dimension.

Another point of the New Testament space and time semantics is the Logos as the outward sign or form. This means that the semantic content as God's will or saving work is inseparable from the visible or audible form of the Word, which implies Jesus' historical teachings and life. The semantic content of the space and time language cannot be understood without its historical form.

In this sense, our semantic formula of the form and content, and vice versa, can also be called the semantics of the Incarnation. When we examine the language of Incarnation, we can find that it is abundant in spatial and temporal and value words, which in turn means the dialectic synthesis of the form and content. The value content of God's glory or His presence is also related to the linguistic form of universal communication.

Finally, the semantic content and form of space and time language demand our active response and participation. The lack of this factor makes the semantic structure of the spatio-temporal language invalid. Jesus' message and life cannot be interpreted and understood without his demanding words. Without repentance, Christian loving action, and participating in his crucifixion, God's revealing action and love are meaningless. St. Paul's letters and other New Testament writings always include both the indicative and the imperative. The spatio-temporal language of Christ's Exaltation, that is his Resurrection, Ascension and Enthronement at the right hand of God is not mere triumphant stories on his part. This language of the New Testament text means that it should be interpreted and understood in our concrete historical context, and that we are demanded to participate in his trans-spatial and trans-temporal saving work.

The Word of God and its spatio-temporal semantics and hermeneutics are not for a classroom academic or speculative work. The New Testament language, particularly the spatio-temporal language, is the dynamic theology of the Word. When we realize this dynamic meaning, the semantic distanciation and appropriation of the New Testament text, or the new horizons, which today's new hermeneutical theories stress, can be easily understood.

PART II.   THE ANALYTICAL
EXPOSITION

This Part will mainly include my interpretations of space and time language and spatio-temporal language in the New Testament, through the three storied universe, Parousia and the Ascension story which I have chosen as my case study. Before doing this hermeneutic work, I will examine the characteristics of the New Testament space and time language and its historical context.

Chapter V.

The Place of Space and Time Language in the New Testament Mythology and its Symbolic Characteristics

A. The Place of Space and Time Language

As is well known, one of the most crucial problems of recent New Testament interpretation is the relation between *kerygma* and myth. Bultmann thinks that *kerygma* and myth can be clearly distinguished from each other and can to a degree be separated. Thus he maintains that the myths must be "demythologized", and the *kerygma* stands intact. But "generally speaking, all of Bultmann's opponents agree with one another that it is not. They insist that we cannot separate the proclamation that God acted in Christ from the story of what that action was. If the story is mythological and subject to demythologization, then the same must be said of the *kerygma*. "[1] This controversy is long and widespread. We do not want to be involved in this controversial problem, but one important point must be made clear here: What Bultmann means by 'mythology' corresponds mostly with the language of space and time. Here we have reason to ask, "What is the place of space and time language in the New Testament mythology, and what are its symbolic characteristics?"

It may be unnecessary to repeat Bultmann's mythological language which refers to space and time.[2] It is enough to admit that for him the primary *skandalon* is the problem of the space and time language, such as 'God is in heaven, '"Christ will come at the last day,' 'His ascension," etc. Such language can be divided roughly into three types: spatial, temporal, and spatio-temporal. These three correspond respectively to cosmological, eschatological and Christological categories. As their outstanding examples, we can take the three-storied universe for spatial (cosmological), *parousia* for temporal (eschatological), and Ascension for spatio-temporal (Christological).

These may be diagrammed as follows:

Spatial	Temporal	Spatio-temporal
(3 storied univ.)	(*parousia*)	(ascension story)
- location -	beginning,	His descending,
heaven above	now, end,	His ascending,
earth here,	past, present,	His pre-existence,
hell below,	future, before,	His going to
in, within, at,	after,	heavenly home,
on, beyond,	at the time,	His coming back,
there, place	Lord's Day,	His sitting at the
where, etc.	last day,	right hand of the
- distance -	*kairos, kronos,*	Father,
close to	from the	His coming again
near to,	beginning to	soon,
distant, far	the last, soon,	Heavenly tabernacle,
long, etc.	quickly, suddenly,	Heavenly throne,
- moving -	hope, waiting,	His Resurrection,
from, to, into,	promise, fulfill-	His self-emptiness,
descend, ascend,	ment, temporal,	His post-Resurrectior appearances,
- degree -	succession,	
high, low, deep	eternal, transiency	His Last Judgement

Diagram 4

As can be seen, the language of space and time is predominant in New Testament mythology. In this connection, Urban is right when he says that "all language is primarily spatial - even in the case of our words for time. In so far as reality is represented by language, then, it tends to be spatialized."[3] Next, we must ask, What are the characteristics of the langauge?

B.   The General Characteristics of Space and Time
      Language in New Testament Mythology

As we have already seen, New Testament mythology gets its material mostly from space and time language. In this sense, W. G. Kuemmel may be right when he limits the definition of myth to include only deeds of a divine being in time and space that have definite meaning for man's existence.[4]

Before entering the main discussion, one or two points must be made. First of all it should be admitted that New Testament mythological language has elements in common with other religious language, because the origin of the Christian religion was not an accidental happening. This means that New Testament mythological language can be dealt with as a general religious language such as is seen in many other religions.

Nevertheless, there is a more important factor, which is a peculiarity of the New Testament language, particularly of the New Testament mythology. Amos Wilder in his discussion of early Christian language puts emphasis on its peculiar forms which were deeply determined by the peculiar faith or, as it were, life-orientation of primitive Christians. To show the relation between the faith and the language, Wilder compares the relation of content and form to the relation of the shape of an axe and its function.[5] This can be roughly applicable to the New Testament mythology, particularly to the space and time language.

As to the characteristics of the forms or expressions in the context of space and time, we first shall discuss them generally:

a) *Dramatic Factor*

There is no doubt that religious language is dramatic, but this is still more true of its mythological language. Thus, New Testament myths should be defined as dramatic stories in symbolic language about God and his relation to men and the world.[6] Professor Macquarrie says that "the narrative or dramatic form is basic to myth. A story is concrete and particular, so that myth stands in this regard at the opposite extreme from the abstract generalizing language of science."[7] Then, what does dramatic mean? According to Urban, "in its primary meaning the dramatic is concerned with representation of human action, although non-human action, both of the gods and of nature, may be included insofar as the latter are anthropomorphized."[8] "Dramatic language is not primarily the language of emotion, although emotion is always present, but rather of will and action."[9]

In this light, we can show some examples of the New Testament drama in the context of space and time. But in order to do so, it is necessary to say something about the Hebrew tradition. The primary character, dramatic or narrative, of the form of mythological language of the New Testament is to be found in traditional Hebrew thought and language, which, while symbolic, in particular, is strikingly effective in its dramatic expression. In the Old Testament the cosmic drama of creation reveals God's redemptive action (will) and shows His shaping of space and time: "*In the beginning* (time) *God* (hero of drama) *created* (action, will) *the heaven and earth* (space)"; the historical drama of God's transaction with the primal man - dialogue type - is presented with materials of space and time relations: *in the garden of Eden* (space), *in the midst of the garden* (space--concreteness of dramatic story), *walking in the garden* (moving in space), "Where are you?'' (space) "God sent him forth from the garden" (space), *in the cool of the day* (time), *all the days of your life* (time), *"till you return to ground, for out of it you were taken"* (spatio-temporal), *"to dust you shall return"* (time), etc.[10] There are many examples of such biblical drama in the Old Testament, but for our purpose here is only to show the historical background of the New Testament drama. Therefore let us turn to New Testament examples; the presentation of them will be more effective in diagrammed form than in literary description. For this, three typical dramatic stories will be used: Lazarus and the rich man (Lk. 16:19-31), the Transfiguration (Mk.9:2-9), and the Ascension (Acts 1:6-11).

Characters		Dialogue	Action	Image (symbol)
Lazarus and the rich man	Abraham, Lazarus, rich man	Abraham with the rich man	angels' carrying Lazarus up	-spatio-temporal - ex. 'after their death' (time), 'the Abraham's bosom far off' (space-- height imagery), 'lifts up his eye' (height), 'in your lifetime' (time), 'a great chasm between' (space), 'this place of torment'(space), etc.
Trans- figura- tion	Jesus the disciples and Moses Elijah	Jesus with Moses, Elijah, with Peter	taking the dis- ciples up the mountain, God's cosmic action	-spatio-temporal - ex. historical succession of Moses, Elijah, Jesus, (time), 'going up high mountain' (space), 'coming down from the mountain' (space), 'it is well that we are here' (space)

Ascen-sion	Jesus, disciples, two men	Jesus with the disciples, angel's promise	Jesus' lifting up, disciple looking up	-spatio-temporal - ex. question about times or seasons (time) 'to the end of the earth' (space), 'as they were looking on' (space), 'he was lifted up' (space), 'while they were gazing into heaven' (space), 'why do you stand looking into heaven?' (space), 'Jesus, who was taken up from you into hea-ven' (space), 'will come --' (time)

Diagram 5

The above examples are only three of many which can be found in New Testament mythology. But these three are enough to show what the dramatic factor is. Briefly, the material of the mythology is almost wholly taken from the language of space and time. This fact can be confirm-ed by dramatic stories, such as the post-Resurrection ap-pearances of Jesus, our High Priest who has gone into heaven, or the new heaven of the last two chapters of the Revelation.

b) *Evocative Factor*

The second characteristic of myth is evocative. Pro-fessor Macquarrie writes, "It is a language with several levels, as it were, and its meaning is not to be read on the surface. We can put this another way by saying that in myth, the connotations of words bulk more largely than their denotations."[11] We know that this occurs particularly in poetic expressions, but this is still more true of religious language because most religious language is a crystallization of human emotive elements which are produced in the tension between incompleteness and ideality.

Then, let us take some illustrations from New Testament mythology, particularly spatial and temporal language. These evocative expressions are mostly terms which are transformed symbolically. For instance, 'light', 'cloud', 'demon', 'angel'-superficial observation would not recognize either that these words have space and time relations or that they have symbolical transformation. It is enough here for us to point out that these terms carry with them, in the language of myth, the wealth of associations which had gathered round these things in the life of the people who produced the myths.

Here are some more examples: 'heaven and earth,' 'holy spirit', 'hell', 'word', 'the Lord's Day', 'sun', 'moon', '*Maran-atha* ','heavenly bread', 'tabernacle', 'son', 'Jerusalem', 'twelve', 'at the right hand', 'peace', 'deep', 'sea', 'Abraham', 'Messiah', 'bride', 'sitting upon the throne', 'Alpha and Omega', 'the water of life', 'seven', 'glory', 'mountain', 'Lamb', 'the tree of life'. We have not presented all possible examples, for there are too many. What is important here is that these words are all compacted with the significance of emotive life-situations and the significant fact is that in this original form they are spatio-temporal language.

c) *Supernatural Factor*

It is not surprising that mythological language has to do with the supernatural, because the content of myth itself deals with supramundane and superhuman events-- for instance, the many miracle stories of the Old and New Testaments, the voices from heaven, Christ's descent into Hades and His Ascension into the heavenly place, His coming again, the cosmic change at the Last day, etc.

The supernatural factor has an almost direct and literal relation with space and time. In other words, it takes the language of space and time as sensible truth, and transcends it. For instance, angels fly away irrespective of space, and the risen Christ appears in disregard of space and time. This element of mythological language is open to criticism from both the theological and the scientific points of view. In particular, Bultmann's criticism of objectifying language is against this aspect of mythology. Yet we should acknowledge with Professor Macquarrie that the conception of the supernatural, even as we find it in myth, cannot just be swept aside, because it pointed to aspects of man's being-in-the-world which we must either find ways to reinterpret, or else frankly acknowledge that we have lapsed into a positivism in which any kind of religious faith and, in particular, any recognizable form of Christianity have become impossible."[12]

In this connection, the statement of Herbert Richardson is noteworthy. He writes that "man's intellectual development has moved from an undifferentiated to a differentiated kind of thinking. It is not the case that primitive thinking is wholly mythical. Rather, in primitive thinking, empirical descriptions, rational hypotheses, and myths all interpret one another in an undifferentiated way."[13] Anyway, it should be acknowledged that in the supernatural element, there is a numinous, powerful entity.

d) *Communal Factor*

This means that a mythology has its social or communal dimension. Professor Macquarrie rightly points out that "myth does not become a myth until it has been adopted by the community; a private story might circulate as a legend, but when we are told of a myth, we surely mean a story that has become formative in the history of a community and which helps to constitute the identity of that community."[14] He also says that "myth serves not only as a cohesive force in the community-- perhaps by telling a story of its origin such as will give it standing and significance--but also as a kind of basic ideology, in relation to which the various events that happen in the community's history can be referred and explained. Even modern and progressive nations have some core of stories or ideas that perform a function similar to that of the old tribal mythologies."[15]

We would say that this is true, particularly in the context of spatial and time relations. Some illustrations will make this clearer. An example can be taken from this author's country. A typical myth of the Korean people is that of Tan-Kun. It has served as a cohesive force in their national life. Tan-Kun was the first king of Korea, whose birth was told as a mythical story. His father was the son of the heavenly King, who had mercy on the world; he descended from the heavenly father, and took his wife, who was an incarnation of a bear and who wanted to become human. Her desire was achieved when, according to the test of the son of the heavenly King, she completed the hundred days of austerities in a cave. This is a simplification of the story, but the important thing here is that we should notice the space and time relations. The same can be said of Shinto, a Japanese myth, which also tells about the heavenly origin of a national god. This truth is almost universal in religious history, but this communal factor of space and time language is more evident in biblical writings. Typical examples are to be found in the stories of Christ's Ascension, and His high priesthood in heaven in the Epistle to the Hebrews, where the ideal hero of the early Christian community transcends space and time. In a wider sense, the imagery of a heavenly banquet, in the Gospels and in Pauline eschatology, and the seer's New Heaven, all originated in the faith-situation of the early Christian community.

C.   The Two Symbolic Characteristics of Space and
        Time Language in New Testament Mythology

In the preceding section, we discussed four general characteristics of New Testament mythology, particularly as related to space and time. But it should be noted that the four factors cannot be independent of the two characteristics of symbolic expression, viz., the denotative and the limitative characteristics. Here attention should be paid to the word 'symbolic', by which I mean the 'intentional' element in the term. The primary sense of the words 'symbol' or 'symbolism' should be found in its purposeful, intentional element. This is distinct from myth, which remains at the level of immediacy, which means "the inner attitude to myth, which was different among those who really thought mythically from what it is among us who can recognize myth as myth."[16]

In this light we will consider the characteristics of symbolism; but before doing so it is necessary to present a diagram of certain characteristics of symbolism.

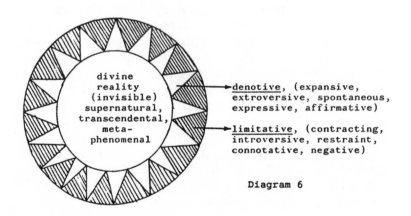

divine reality (invisible) supernatural, transcendental, meta-phenomenal

denotive, (expansive, extroversive, spontaneous, expressive, affirmative)

limitative, (contracting, introversive, restraint, connotative, negative)

Diagram 6

Diagram 6

a) *Denotative Characteristic*

As shown, the function of symbolism is to be found in the two ways by which it reveals invisible reality: denotative and limitative. The former is expansive, spontaneous, and the latter, contracting, restrained. Some examples will be helpful in understanding this. For both features, a good example is the biblical idea about 'heaven.' 'Heaven' is denotative. The idea is taken from spatial language, and its innate intention is to reveal God's transcendence through height imagery; God is 'above.' This denotative characteristic tries to explain innate reality in empirical, sensuous language, sometimes in vivid, concrete, visual images, as seen in the Ascension story.[17] Sometimes heaven is expressed (or denoted) in the plural form like 'heaven and the heaven of heavens':
ὁ οὐρανὸς καὶ ὁ οὐρανὸς τῶν οὐρανῶν
(Dt. 10:14, I Kings 8:27, Ps. 148:4), 'all the heavens':   πάντων τῶν οὐρανῶν   (Eph. 4:10, RV), 'up to the third heaven':   ἕως τρίτου οὐρανοῦ   (II Cor. 12:2), 'in the heavenly places':   ἐν τοῖς ἐπουρανίοις   (Eph. 1:3, 20, 2:6, 3:10, 6:12), the idea of Christ as the greatest High Priest who 'has passed through the heavens':
διεληλυθότα τοὺς οὐρανούς
(Heb. 4:14), 'exalted above the heavens':
ὑψηλότερος τῶν οὐρανῶν γενόμενος
(Heb. 7:26). In New Testament mythology, these denotative elements are found mostly in the stories bearing Christological themes, like the Trans-figuration, Resurrection appearances, Ascension, etc. For this reason, the denotative characteristic has its primary relationship with the dramatic and supernatural factors of mythological language.

b) *Limitative Characteristic*

A limitative characteristic is, in a strict sense, not separable from the denotative, its counterpart, because reality, which they both symbolize in different ways, can be conveyed to us only when the two elements operate in reciprocal relation.

An example can be taken from the concept of heaven. In its denotative characteristic, 'heaven' was used to denote the peculiar abode of Deity, with which the ideas of elevation, majesty, glory, power, holiness, unchangeableness are associated. Nevertheless, heaven is also described as incapable of containing Him, and the prophets declare His greatness to be such as to surpass all the bounds of space and all ideas of residence within the limits even of the heaven of heavens. (Is. 40:12, 66:1, cf. I Kings 8:27). In many things the biblical books show a reverent reserve.

This is also true of the eschatological use of 'heaven.' In many passages the quality of the changeless and enduring is ascribed to 'heaven', especially in contrast with the mutable earth and the perishable life of man (Job 11:21, Ps. 72:5, 7, 17, Jer. 31:35, etc.). But heaven is also exhibited as an aspect of the changeful and transitory, as contrasted with the changeless being and eternal years of God Himself (Ps. 102:25-27; Is. 51:6). This limitative element of symbolism reaches its climax in dealing with the Heavenly sanctuary where God's Presence is not localized or temporalized, but lives in the perpetual light of the presence. In this sense the limitative characteristic can be said to be a check or warning against physicalizing or materializing of the transcendent, spiritual reality.

In conclusion, we will add two quotations. Citing C. Jung, Urban writes, "The attitude of symbolism in general consists in endowing an occurrence, an event in space and time, whether great or small, with a meaning to which greater value and significance is given than belong to it in its pure actuality or existence."[18]

Nevertheless, the spiritual object characterized by the symbol is not only affirmative but negative. That is to say, the object 'is so,' but it is also 'not so.' Professor Macquarrie says that "simply to affirm an analogue or symbol is to fall into that over-literalness which, if we are applying the image of God, leads into an attitude of idolatry. Whatever symbol or analogy is affirmed must be at the same time denied."[19]

Chapter VI

The Symbolic Meaning
of Space and Time Language
in New Testament Mythology

In the preceding chapters, we discussed some modern hermeneutic problems of space and time language in the New Testament mythology, and the characteristics of this language.

With these accounts as background, our purpose in this chapter is to inquire into the meaning of this space and time language. Here a question may arise, 'What is the nature of meaning?' This question would demand a long and complicated discussion about semantic theories.[1] We will simply state our position here about problem. It is characteristic of meaning to be universal in its relationship to communication. In order to understand this, it is necessary to quote Urban's statements: "There is a sense in which everything denoted by language is universalized. Whatever particular sign is named, the very act of naming, of speaking, transforms and universalizes it."[2] The further consideration of the universal as a *sine qua non* of semantic meaning belongs to other contexts--the relation of the universal to communication. Communication, either overt or latent, is, we have found, implied in all linguistic meaning. Communication, however, implies the universal. This fact has been expressed by Sapir in the following way:

> The elements of language, the symbols that are significant of experience, must be associated with delimited classes of experiences, rather than with the single experiences themselves. Only so is communication possible. For the single experience lodges in the individual consciousness and is strictly incommunicable. To be communicated it must needs be referred to a class that is tacitly accepted by the community as an identity.[3]

It is entirely clear that, just as the universal is the *sine qua non* of semantic meaning, so it is the *sine qua non* of communication. Strictly speaking, individual experiences cannot be communicated. It is equally clear that the universal must be at least tacitly accepted by the community. Mutual acknowledgement of the universal is the condition of communication.

With these accounts of semantic ideas as our basic principles, we shall analyze the symbolic structures of the given texts: the three-storied universe, *parousia*, and the Ascension story. First, we first shall consider briefly their historical contexts.

A.   Spatial Language of New Testament Mythology

Case study: 'Three-storied Universe'

1) *Its Historical Environment*

As we have already seen, the three-storied universe of which Bultmann spoke means the primitive conception of the world as being structured in three levels: heaven, earth, and hell. God and his angels live in heaven; and the under-world is hell, the place of torment. The earth is where God and his angels meet with Satan and his demons. Bultmann says that all this is mythological language that is derived from the mythology of Jewish apocalyptic and Gnostic redemption myths. We think that it is not to be doubted that the three-storied universe is a mythological conception of the pre-scientific age (Ps. 148:4, 24:2, 104:5, Gen. 7:11, etc.). The origin of this cosmological myth is to be found in the cosmological imageries of Babylon and other ancient Near Eastern countries.[4] For instance, the suggestive power of the ancient mythology remains, in which the cosmic world came into being out of primitive chaos with a primeval struggle in which the high God smote 'the deep' (Tiamat, Tehom, Gen. 1:2; Rahab, Tsa. 51:9f., Ps. 89:9f., Leviathan, Ps. 104:26; Job, 41:1).[5] Nevertheless the ancient imagery has been much 'demythologized'[6] in Hebrew faith. An example of this can be found in the Hebrews' conception of 'sky'. While Mesopotamians retained the conception of a divine bow hung in the sky, the Hebrews identified it with the rainbow and not, as did the Babylonians, with a constellation. They took it to be a sign of God's promise not to send another flood (Gen. 9:12-15), rather than, as in other cultures, his victorious weapon hung in the sky as a warning to future upstarts.[7] We can take this as a tendency of spatial imagery to become temporal. This type of development is in accordance with principles of linguistic symbolism.[8]

In Hebrew thought, the spiritual expressed itself in the physical, and natural events were interpreted in terms of temporal images, that is, the hopes and expectations which came to existential significance for them.[9] As seen in any kind of symbolic development of reality, Hebrew symbolism also had its roots in empirical lives. Expressions like 'a pillar of cloud,' 'glory,' 'God's presence,' 'His anger,' etc., are all from daily living and daily language. The same is to be said of their spatial words like 'deep', 'Sheol', 'earth', 'heaven', etc. With the rise of apocalyptic writings, Hebrew symbolism often took the form of figurative and even fantastic elaboration, as is seen in the weird and bizarre imagery which was brought in so as to describe past and future history, or the divisions of heaven.

All of these are examples, in historical context, of the three-storied universe. But here the problem of another background might be posited, namely, a Gnostic background.[10] Bultmann writes, "Gnostic terminology places its stamp mainly on the words and discourse source which presumably underlies them; rather, it runs through the whole Gospel and the Epistles."[11]

We may need not engage ourselves in the controversy of whether or not Bultmann's hypothesis is right,[12] but we can note that his discussion of the '*Urmensch*' myth can be illustrated by a scheme of space and time: 'heavenly world,' 'the highest god,' 'come down,' 'heavenly home,' 'heavenly journey,' etc.[13]

In the preceding paragraphs, we have seen that the background of New Testament mythology lies in the spatial relations. But particularly in Hebrew tradition, spatial language was in the process of transformation into that of temporal relations. The determining factor in this process was the Hebrews' faith in God as Creator. This means that outward form (expression) was determined by inner reality. In this sense A. Wilder seems to be right when he says that the forms of the early Christian literature "are evidently deeply determined by the faith or life-orientation that produced them."[14]

Before we can turn to the symbolic meaning, we shall outline the symbolic structure of the meaning of the three-storied universe.

2) *Symbolic Development of Spatial Language*

symbolic development vertical division of spatial language	spatial signification $\longrightarrow$	qualitatives of symbolism (despatializing)
Heaven (above)	*in* heaven, *in* Abraham's bosom, *between* us & you, sat *upon throne,*	height, elevation, majesty, glory, light, power, honour, holiness,

	lifted up his eyes *to* heaven, *up, above,* etc.	unchangeableness, white, pure, happiness, Father's home, His Presence, blessed,
	angel *was sent from,* the angel *went away,* from them to heaven, *pass from* here to, none may *cross from, ascending* to my Father,	life, eternal,
Earth, world (here)	*on, at, in, between here, there,*	good and evil, happiness and sorrow, hope and despair,
Hell (below)	*in* Hades, *deep,* bottomless *pit, below,* *down,* *to* Hell, *was thrown into* the Lake of fire, *descend to* Hades,	torment, wickedness, evil, false, darkness, despair, sin, death, curse, hopeless, eternal death,

Diagram 7

3) The Symbolic Meaning of the Spatial Language

The above diagram is intended to show that, according to the law of language development, spatial significations of the New Testament mythological language develop "from copy to analogy and from analogy to symbol".[15] In other words, spatial signification is to be interpreted as the symbol for non-spatial relations, which is filled with 'spiritual content.' Otherwise the language must inevitably 'distort reality.'

Now, let us interpret the spatial language of the threestoried universe. First of all, as has been shown, words or phrases of spatial signification are despatialized in terms of qualitative language; for instance, 'God is in heaven' is related to images like majesty, light, white, etc.; 'Hell' is related to those like torment, evil, sin, death, etc. The former has positive content, the latter negative. This process of despatializing is necessary in order to reveal the universal meanings of language, which are related to the 'disclosedness' of human existence. The primary experience of human beings is a consciousness of the sensuous world of space. Heaven is related to 'clear up,' 'high,' 'light,' 'white cloud,' 'vastness,' 'mystery,' etc. In connection with the sun or other heavenly bodies, or with high mountains, and also with the image of a king elevated above ordinary people, the 'height' image is connected with value words like majesty, power, etc. These words are analogical and symbolic ways of describing man's existence. When man is conscious of height, vastness, and light, he understands himself to be a very tiny, limited, and dark (in the moral sense) being. Nevertheless, man's consciousness of his limitations implies a desire to attain a limitless, complete, happy state. His language passes through symbolic transformation to qualitative content which connotes the ideality or spiritual purpose of his existence.

Now we can apply this meaning of the symbolic language to the New Testament context. The semantic problem of 'heaven' or 'God is in heaven' is related to the question, 'Where are you?'. In both cases, the outward forms of language are sensuous and empirical, but their innate contents are transformed into language of value and weight, that is, spiritual contents. It should be noted here that the mysterious Being 'heavenly Father' is taken primarily from the sensuous experience of space, and is then transformed by the existential questions 'Where are you?'

or 'Where am I?'. This means that its symbolic meaning has both cosmic and existential significance. Thus the phrase 'God is in heaven' is to be understood in the light of these two dimensions. This is true of almost every religious terminology, but it is particularly important in the New Testament language about heaven, which should be understood in the context of Christological terms. These will be discussed in the last chapter which deals with spatio-temporal language. What we can say here is that the language of space was valued and deepened into meaningful dimensions by the Christological confession of the early Church.

To say a few words may be sufficient about 'hell'. As we said above, 'hell' is only a negative counterpart of the 'heaven' image. Thus its qualitative words or phrases are contrasted with those of 'heaven', as seen in the words 'deep', 'torment', 'darkness', 'sin', 'death'. But here, a point must be noted about the moral character of the 'hell' image. It means that, while the primary material of the 'heaven' image is taken from the sensuous world of space, that of 'hell' comes from constituents of the conscious life as man knows it within himself, and from the emotions, acts of will, and values of others.[16] These elements of our conscious life are developed through symbolic transformation into a moral language with terms like 'guilty', 'sin', 'punishment', 'torment', 'death'. Here, images of physical things such as 'valley of Hinnom', 'prison', 'depth of the sea', 'bottomless pit', are taken as the material for symbolic transformation.

In conclusion the spatial language of the three-storied universe has its ultimate meaning in the cosmic and existential dimension. Our human life in this world is that of this experience.

B.   Temporal Language of New Testament Mythology

Case study: Parousia

1) *Its Historial Environment*

The concept of *parousia* comes from a Hebrew-Jewish background.[17] The Old Testament people, whose national consciousness was shaped by the 'mighty acts' of the Exodus, awaited a further divine deliverance in the future. This expectation is referred to in Old Testament passages describing the 'Day of the Lord,' the 'latter days,' 'that day,' etc. During the intertestamental period this many-coloured hope was modified by apocalyptic thought and by the increasingly widespread belief in a personal Messiah as the agent of God's deliverance. No single pattern of Messianic expectation emerged. Some writers regarded the Messiah as the reviver of the Davidic dynasty (e.g. Pss. Sol. 17-18). To others, he was the apocalyptic Son of man.[18] Still others expected no personal Messiah at all. Political, ethical, and apocalyptic ideas mingled in confusing fashion. The common factor was belief in a divine, eschatological intervention occurring at the end of history. While New Testament faith asserted that in Jesus the Messiah had already come, His further coming in glory was awaited: i.e., the *parousia*. This expectation was the continuation of the Old Testament hope.[19]

Now we are faced with the difficult problem of how to reconcile these two seemingly contradictory points of view. The problem must be dealt with in detail. In order to do this, first of all the concept of *parousia* must be defined. *Parousia* is typical temporal language in New Testament mythology, and is related to futuristic images: the second coming of Christ, His Last Judgment, the Last Day, etc. The original usage of the word, *parousia*, in classical and *koine* Greek, was in the general sense of 'presence' but its meaning became extended to include also the idea of 'arrival' or 'coming' (cf. Neh. 2:6; Jud. 10:18; II Mac. 8:12; III Macc. 3:17). H.K. McArthur says that of the twenty-four occurrences in the New Testament, six show this wider meaning[20] (e.g. I Cor. 16:17; II Cor. 7:6-7, 10:10; Phil. 1:26, 2:12). In this connection the historical revelation of Christ can be discussed. This is the question about the presentation of Christ's salvation, to which the adverb 'no longer'   οὐκέτι   can be applied, whereas the adverb 'not yet'   οὔπω   became attached to the concept of futuristic eschatology.

When one reads the New Testament, one gains the strong impression that the authors believed that they were writing about, and under the impact of, a decisive event in history. Some examples of this can be found throughout the New Testament: Kingdom of God (Mk. 1:15; Lk. 11:20; Mt. 12:28), the fulfillment of Messianic expectation (Mt. 11:2-6; Lk. 7:18-23), the Holy Spirit as an eschatological event (Lk.1:35; Mk. 1:10), exorcisms[21] (Mk. 3:27: Mt. 12:27), the crucifixion of the Messiah as a struggle against the evil spirits of the cosmos (I Cor. 2:8; Heb. 2:14), the Johannine emphasis on the fulfillment of Messianic expectations in Christ (Jn. 5:24, 3:16, etc.), and the Pauline thought of the new creation in Christ (II Cor. 2:15, 4:3f). In particular, Paul's passage about present salvation is worthy to be quoted: "Behold, now is the acceptable time; behold now is the day of salvation.":

ἰδοὺ νῦν καιρὸς εὐπρόσδεκτος,
ἰδοὺ νῦν ἡμέρα σωτηρίας   (II
Cor. 6:2b).

Nevertheless, the New Testament speaks not only of what has happened in the past, or what is taking place in the present. It also looks forward to a fulfillment in the future, to a consummation of what has been begun. For instance, although Christ saw Satan fall like lightning from heaven (Lk. 19:18), Paul much later knew that Satan was still at work on the earth (I Cor. 7:5; II Cor. 2:11, etc.). From one standpoint the victory was won, but from the other the battle was still raging. Jesus' teachings were also largely eschatological in character (Mt. 25:14-30; Lk. 29:12-27; Mt. 25:1-13, Mt. 25:11f). The early Christians' identification of Jesus' Second Coming with the coming Son of Man, Paul's futuristic aspect of salvation, Epistle to Hebrews, I and II Peter, and Jude, all speak of a future fulfillment. Even the Johannine writings, in which salvation is almost exclusively conceived as a present reality, and in which the judgment is understood as taking place in the present, refer to a future appearing and a future day of judgment (Jn. 6:39, 40, 44, 54, 8:24, 12:48, 13:36, 14:2f.).

In the above paragraphs we have been aware of seemingly contradictory points of view. In order to discuss the resulting problem we turn next to an analysis of the structure of temporal language.

2) *Symbolic Development of Temporal Language*

a)   Comparison of the parousia with general time
      Consciousness

        i) general concept of time

endless time   ---- time succession ----

--- before ---- now ---- after ---

---- past -------- present -------- future ----

--- earlier --------   -------- later ---

Diagram 8

ii) eschatological concept of time

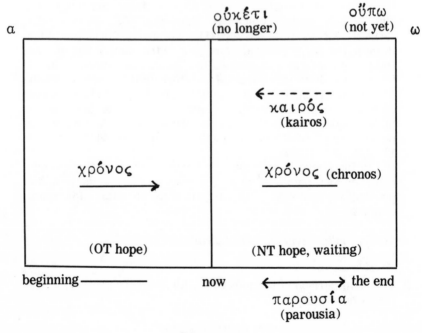

Diagram 9

b)   Symbolic development of parousia language

denotative	limitative	qualitative	(detemporal- ization)
dramatic, super- natural	connotative	personal dimension	ultimate value or meaning
signs of His coming (Mt. 24:3)	present salvation (Jn. 5:24)	to watch	salvation
His sudden coming (Mk. 13:)	eschato- logical, Holy Spirit	take heed, to prepare	new creation, eternal life
the promise of His coming	fulfillment, Messianic expectation in Christ		
darkening of the sun and moon	light or glory in Christ	abide in Christ	changeless- ness, joy
false prophets	truth in Christ		eternal truth
His Second Coming	His Incarnation	establish your hearts	reconciliation, love
cosmic changes	His crucifixion	believe in Christ	eternal life
time succession	no time	rejoice	eternal light

Diagram 10

3) *Symbolic Meaning of Temporal Language*

The above diagrams show how different the forms of *parousia* language are from those of temporal language in general, and they demonstrate that the symbolic meaning of *parousia* is to be sought in the universal dimension of the language which is developed through its symbolic transformation.

As shown in the diagram, *parousia* language is characterized by its cosmic significance and its psychological and ethical elements. *Parousia* language includes cosmic dimensions, like supernatural events and new creation, and also personal, internal dimensions like warning and exhortation. This means that *parousia* language is determined strongly by the life-situation of the early Christian community which was Christological in character. For this reason the ultimate meaning of the *parousia* language will be examined in the last chapter of this part, where Christological language will be dealt with in terms of spatio-temporal language. Before this can be done, however, we should consider the essential character and function of *parousia* language.

First of all, *parousia* language is distinguished, by its negation of time, from other temporal language, in which the form of 'being' is designated as succession, as time.[22] A typical example of negation is the expression 'Alpha and Omega.' This means that Christian faith is in the Lordship of Christ that transcends time and history, and in which our consciousness of constant change and nothingness, transiency and destiny in the temporal world, gain the dimension of dynamic meaning. When we say that Christ is α and ω, first of all we suggest the negative sense of the general consciousness of endless time succession, and at the same time we affirm that our Christian life has a meaningful origin and a meaningful goal. Nevertheless, our present life is tinged with uncertainty. Even though we are now living in the day of salvation, no one can say that the present situation is complete, final, blessed, or eternal. Here we have reason to ask what is the dimension of 'chronos': time.[23] This includes promise, expectation, hope, His Coming again, the Last Day, Last Judgment, *Maran-atha*. Such a futuristic dimension is unavoidable as long as we human beings stay in this temporal world. Although we try to reach meta-temporal reality, that is to say, eternity[24] and try to negate the physical, literal expression, our human language is too limited to copy or symbolize the complex ideality of time. For this reason, in temporal language the negative element of symbolism is strong. Here the Seer's passage can be quoted: "And night shall be no more; they need no light of lamp or sun, for the Lord God will be their light, and they shall reign for ever and ever" (Rev. 22:5).

needs existential interpretation.[2] But we should try to discover the more significant truth in the Ascension, particularly in the story of Acts 1:9-11, even though the story has been treated more negatively than have other references to the exalted Christ in the New Testament because of Acts' physical description of the Ascension. But if we understand the more recent scholarly studies in Lucan theology,[3] and the dramatic, poetic description at the beginning of Acts, we will notice that it includes more significant meaning. We can prove this through the interpretation of its historical, and symbolic meaning and particularly through linguistic analysis of the structure of its symbolic language. Our conclusion is that the symbolic language, in Acts 1, shows us the essential truth of our Christological confession, that is, our ultimate credal language of the sovereign Christ in terms of space and time.

A.   Its Historical Environment

With Eric Dinkler we can divide the myths of the New Testament into three types.[4] These are cosmological, eschatological, and Christological, with outstanding examples representative of each of these divisions: the three-storied universe for the cosmological, the *parousia* for the eschatological, and the Ascension story for the Christological.

The Ascension or Exaltation of Jesus Christ as a Christological myth is a product of the primitive Church, made after the events of the Cross and the Resurrection of Jesus Christ, and used for the interpretation of the meaning of those events. The references to the myth are made in various forms in the New Testament: 'to take up' ($\dot{\alpha}\nu\alpha\lambda\alpha\beta\dot{\alpha}\nu\epsilon\iota\nu$ Acts 1:2, 1:11; I Tim. 3:16), 'to exalt' (Acts 2:33, 5:31), ' to sit down at the right hand of God' ($\varkappa\alpha\theta\dot{\iota}\zeta\epsilon\iota\nu$ $\dot{\epsilon}\nu$ $\delta\epsilon\xi\iota\tilde{\alpha}$ $\alpha\dot{\upsilon}\tauo\tilde{\upsilon}$ Eph. 1:20; Heb. 1:3, 10:12), 'to go up or ascend' ($\dot{\alpha}\nu\alpha\beta\alpha\dot{\iota}\nu\epsilon\iota\nu$ Acts 2:34; John 3:13, 6:52, 20:17;   Eph.   4:8-10).   The restyled version of the resurrection-Ascension sequence found in the Lucan writings is very impressive. But, as F.C. Grant said, the earliest tradition regards the Resurrection and the Ascension as one event.[5] Alan Richardson thinks that the fourth Gospel, which dates the gift of the Spirit (John 20:22) on the evening of Easter Sunday (John 20:19), after Jesus had already ascended to the Father (John 20:17), and had returned in his glorified body, probably preserves the more primitive understanding of the matter. St. Matthew does not mention the Ascension, nor does the shorter ending of St. Mark.

Today it is generally recognized that the report of the Resurrection and Ascension (Mk. 16:9-20) found in the majority of the manuscripts and versions was not a part of the original Gospel. There seems to be nothing in the Old Testament to parallel the Ascension of Jesus. Some scholars think that the nearest manifestations were the 'translation' of Enoch and the assumption of Elijah, while others try to find the sources in Gnostic myth or in some ancient myths of divine ascension.

We do not need to spend much time on this question, for the sources of the story are, for our purposes, of little importance. Far more important for us is to know the situation in which the story was crystallized as Christological language, to know its *Sitz im Leben*. As Jean Danielou says, the Ascension story may be likely from the liturgical usage of the primitive Church and expresses His Heavenly Kingship as had been prefigured in the liturgy of the Royal Psalms. Father Danielou said that "Psalm cx is an essential source for the theology of the Ascension, and the New Testament itself is the first to apply it in this way. As a description of the Ascension, a verse of this Psalm is found incorporated in the oldest profession of Christian faith, the discourse of St. Peter on the day of Pentecost (Acts 2:30-35).[6] He also points out that Psalm xxiv, which describes a procession entering into the temple in Jerusalem, was applied in the Epistle to the Hebrews, in which the entrance of Christ into the heavenly

Temple at the Ascension was said to be the fulfillment in Christ of what the temple cult had already proclaimed. This is supported by the evidence of priestly kingship given at a rite of kingly anointing that was part of the liturgy of the temple.[7]

We should also notice that the liturgical song of Psalm XXIV, "Lift up the gates of heaven, let them open and the king of glory shall enter in," was employed in the Christian liturgy of the early Church. We might ask, Is the prophetic interpretation well founded? Does it not rest to some extent on arbitrary connections? But for the present discussion this is not an important question, for even though the original meaning of the Psalm was not Messianic, but merely pointed to an historical king, its Christological interpretation preserves its own value in the language of the Christian creeds. This is more true of its symbolic meaning, which transforms the reference from a particular historical occurrence into terms that are applicable to universal values.

B.   Symbolic Meaning of the Ascension Story

In the above paragraphs, we have seen that the Ascension story was related to the liturgical situation in which dramatic, pictorial, and sometimes poetic expressions of language and action were used as means of conveying their innate meaning. This fact becomes more clear when we consider St. Luke's elaborate theological scheme. We may call it a symbolic language, as Professor John Macquarrie writes,[8] when we use the word 'symbol' as a conscious or intended character detached from the myth of the immediacy stage. Unlike other writers, St. Luke gives a much more detailed account of the events of the Ascension and the coming of the Spirit, and he lays stress on a period of 'waiting' between the Resurrection and the coming of the Spirit (Luke 24:49, 53). He alone among the New Testament writers itemizes and dates the Resurrection and Ascension of Christ, and the coming of the Spirit, as separate historical events.

Alan Richardson says that the Church has constructed her calendar upon this model, and for the purpose of the due liturgical observances of the truths of our salvation it has proved valuable beyond estimation.[9] I think, however, that the truth is vice versa. St. Luke's composition was modelled upon the earliest Church's liturgical calendar, because his crystallized Ascension story, with its Markan addition, was not the earliest tradition. At any rate it is enough for us here to recognize that the story is of liturgical and symbolic character.

We know how vivid and pictorial the description of Acts 1:9-11 is. But we also must see the author's intention, which appears in his beautiful 'image-language.' With this image language, the writer attempts to tell his readers something more important than the other evangelists attempted. We can regard this as his symbolism, found in his interpretation of the Christ event in terms of space and time, which we will examine below.

1) *The Symbolic Structure of the Ascension*

In order to understand St. Luke's Christological meaning, a structure of the story is presented in a diagrammatic form.[10]

symbolic character factors of myth	denotative	limitative
Dramatic factor	hero--Jesus, Character (Jesus, disciples, angels,	Remodelness of Ascension materials for Christological meaning (in terms of the spatio-temporal process)

dialogue (Jesus-
disciples)

action (ascending,
gazing into
heaven, angels'
prophetic
promise)

Evocative factor	Cloud (of an Epiphany, Lk.9:34, Mk. 14:62, Dan. 7:13) White robe (of baptismal use of early Church and witnesses of glorious king)	much less evocative forms than other ascension stories (Old Testament or apocalyptic writings)
Supernatural factor	Scene of Christ ascending into heaven, Two men dressed in white and their prophecy	much less in fantastic character than other stories (e.g. the letter of James, Jung, Codex)
Communal factor	Ascension stories were adopted in ancient time; cf. Gen. 5:24, Jub.4:23, Ecclus. 44:16, I Enoch 39:3ff, Heb. 11:5, Mk. 9:2-8	use for liturgical community

Diagram 11

The diagram is intended to give a structural understanding
of the symbolism in the Ascension story (Acts 1:9-11). As shown
in the diagram, the story is composed of four factors which indicate the formal characteristics of myth, and of two elements

which exhibit the internal characteristics of symbolism. Attention should be drawn particularly to the latter because it suggests St. Luke's theological motif. We should here emphasize St. Luke's symbolical theology. Bultmann thinks that we can explain to modern men the real meaning of the story by explaining away its mythological symbolism. A. Richardson says that "there is no reason to think that the New Testament writers were not as conscious as he is of the fact that they were using symbolic language when they spoke of, for example, 'Jesus ascending into heaven or descending into hell.' They could only express their meaning in such symbolic forms, and it is possible for man (except the sophisticated) in every generation to understand quite clearly what they meant. It is incredible that St. Luke, in telling the story of Jesus' Ascension meant the parable to be taken literally; he knew better than we do that religious truth, which passes the frontier of intellectual understanding, can be "grasped only by the faith-inspired human imagination, so that through it men can hear, each in his own language, the proclamation of the mighty works of God."[11] We think that Alan Richardson's criticism of Bultmann's mythological symbolism is generally right, but this is also true of the denotative character of symbolism shown in the diagram; the symbolic element of limitative character must not be overlooked in the story.

We have considered the symbolic structure of the Ascension story. Our understanding of this structure led us to observe a more important symbolic element, which leaves a dominant impression on the whole story, namely, 'a spatio-temporal image.' To this we will now turn our attention.

2) *Spatio-Temporal Symbol*

The influence of the Ascension story of Acts 1:7-9 has been impressive. In spite of the fact that the story is only three verses long, far shorter than many other stories of Christ's exaltation, and that many modern clergy have delivered critical preaching against its literal understanding, why does this story remain so strongly influential among ordinary Christians? Is it merely because they do not understand modern New Testament scholarship? But even critical Christians, if they are serious about the story, will feel something real in the pictorial image. Then what is the reason? We think this is a very important question that has

often been overlooked. Therefore, let us consider the question of
'spatio-temporal' image.

In the Ascension story, we recognize again the two strongly
influential images of space and time. These are described in the
symbolic terms which have been mentioned above. The story
says: 'After he said such and such to his disciples about the
future of Israel' Jesus was lifted up into heaven and two men in
white robes prophesied Jesus' Second Coming ... What is this
spatio-temporal image? Instead we should first ask the question
about the spatial symbol which was described by the spatial
words or phrases, "He was taken up"--- "into the heaven as he
went." (For other references to Christ's exaltation, see
pp.115-116). These can all be called spatial language because they
use such words as 'lift', 'high', 'place' (heaven), 'going up'
(ascending), 'earth', 'heaven.' These images are connected with
other spatial language, 'descending', 'down', 'to hell', 'under the
earth.' All these words and phrases exhibit a symbolic structure,
as follows in the next diagram:

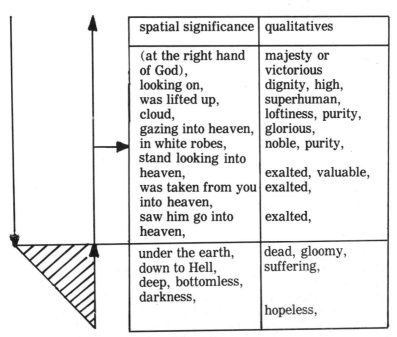

spatial significance	qualitatives
(at the right hand of God), looking on, was lifted up, cloud, gazing into heaven, in white robes, stand looking into heaven, was taken from you into heaven, saw him go into heaven,	majesty or victorious dignity, high, superhuman, loftiness, purity, glorious, noble, purity, exalted, valuable, exalted, exalted,
under the earth, down to Hell, deep, bottomless, darkness,	dead, gloomy, suffering, hopeless,

Diagram 12

In the above diagram we have examined how spatial language is developed, through the meaning of sentences, into image language at the 'story-level' in which mythical language functions. On this matter, Herbert W. Richardson wrote, "The meaning of mythical discourse arises at the level of the total story, the most complex unit of linguistic utterance. The linguistic unit appropriate to myth is not the single word, nor even the sentence, but the story."[12] For Richardson, the meaning of the mythical language at the story level is to be expressed as an image of the story taken as a whole. We think that this idea is applicable to the Ascension story because, in this story, the image of the whole is so real and plays so important a role. Then what is the imagery of the story? Without doubt, it is an image or symbol of spatial sovereignty, expressed as 'height.' Edwyn Bevan is right when, in his book *Symbolism and Belief*, he says, "If there are two characteristics upon which men all over the world, from the earliest stages of traceable human thought, have agreed on attributing to the Chief Being of the universe, they are: height, and length of life."[13] He is also right in saying that the word 'height' should be understood as a qualitative conception like value, or as in the word 'superior.' For instance, when we call God 'The Most High' it means that value belongs to God in a supreme degree. The same is true when we say that 'Christ ascended into heaven.' Our human language has various kinds of qualitative words, mostly adjectival and adverbial. Some are positive and others negative in their expression. For instance, someone is called 'a great man', others cowardly, beautiful or dirty, joyful or sad, gentle or wild sweet or bitter, and so on. These are all qualitative forms. The positive expression provides the concept of value, and superior values as 'high' or 'lofty,' words universally associated with worth and with the divine. Analogous examples can be found in the myth of the Indo-European Sky-God, or the Emperor of the Most High, Sahng-Je (上帝). The last is an ancient concept of the deity in the Far North East.

Now we must return to our main subject, the Ascension, and conclude the discussion of its symbolic meaning. As we have seen, the language of the story was composed with words of spatial signification, and the image of the whole story was 'height,' which indicates supreme quality or value, everywhere in human life. Thus we cannot avoid symbolism to some degree. According to B.H. Throckmorton 'spatial language' is unavoidable because we have no other language and every question about 'where' connotes a place in space.[14] But when we understand the question about the 'where' as symbolical language, then its answer 'He ascended into heaven' or 'at the right hand of God, He sits' should be interpreted in terms of a symbolic meaning, that is, his Lordship, his sovereignty over the cosmic world and man. In this sense it seems right when Oscar Cullmann says "The Lordship began with his Ascension and will end with his return."

Finally, consider temporal language. In the Ascension story we see not only the image of spatial language, 'height', but also the image of the temporal. In a sense the combination of the spatial and temporal images is of further significance in terms of 'spatio-temporal' language. In the story the two men in white robes promise, "Men of Galilee, why do you stand looking into heaven? This Jesus, who was taken up from you into heaven, will come in the same way as you saw him go into heaven." According to G.H.C. Macgregor, the belief in Christ's personal return is one of the central tenets of the earliest creed.[15] In the early New Testament period Christians were radically oriented toward the imminent return of Jesus and the consummation of all things, that is, the passing away of heaven and earth and the coming of the new creation. In this radical orientation toward the *parousia*, Christians saw their lives, faith, and worship ordered toward an immediate divine resolution of all human endeavours. When this resolution did not come to pass as quickly as expected, adjustments were necessary in the Christian conception of time, and in the Christian conception of what was meant by the Second Coming of Jesus. But, we may ask, if, as found in the New Testament *kerygma*, salvation is given, why does the Christian yet hope for it? New Testament writers say that the Kingdom of God *has* come and that it *will* come. This is a paradox, and a burden of the Christian life which the New Testament makes very plain. We do not need to repeat here those questions which have been much discussed in modern New Testament theology. What is important for us here is to understand the symbolic meaning of the temporal language. As shown in the spatial language we can express the symbolic structure of the temporal language as follows:

(Heb. Aleph) α	(Now) νῦν	(Heb. Tau) ω
the first		the last (Rev. 22:13)
the beginning		the end
he who was		he who is to come
from whom are all things	through him	to whom are all things (Rom. 11:36)
who was	who is	who is to come (Rev. 1:8)

Hitherto---now-- henceforth
(Mt. 23:39)   (Mt. 23:39)

kairos ---   chronos [16]

οὐκέτι

οὔπω

waiting for promise
(Acts 1:4)

for consummation
(Rom. 9:19, 23,25)

Diagram 13

We must learn to realize that God is no more in time than He is in space. The application of temporal measures to His life, even though infinite temporal measures, is just as inappropriate as spatial measures. Nevertheless, we try to express His acts in terms of our temporal words of past, present and future. Of all such words, those relating to the future give particularly significant meaning to our human life. For man is best characterized as a creature oriented toward the future, a creature of promise. In his relationship with the past, man is conscious of certain realities of his present, but his meaningful life is still in the future. That is why the early Christians waited for Christ's coming again. The events that they expected to occur in the last days affirmed not only God's final Lordship over history, but his present and past Lordship as well. This means that our human existence, which is conditioned spatially and temporally, wants to go beyond his spatial and temporal finitude and achieve the universal values of trans-spatio and trans-temporal dimension.

The semantic and hermeneutical meaning of the text (Acts 1:6-11) is to bring out the universal value or quality of the ascended Christ whose triumphant saving act is expressed as the spatial image of 'going up' or 'ascension'. What, then, is the value or quality language in the Ascension story? It includes such phrases as eternal heavenly light, almighty power or authority, which are all related to the transcendent language of God's Creation. In this sense, the language of the Exaltation, that is, the risen Christ, ascended Christ, with his present status at God's right hand, expresses the restoration of the original creation, or the regaining of Paradise lost. The language of Ascension is not any historical or objective scientific description, but a faith language, which expresses the revealing knowledge and experience of God's saving act. However, our faith language still uses space and time imageries because we have no any other language than in spatio-temporal terms. Spatio-temporal language expresses our longing for the infinite and ultimate value with terms that are finite. The ineffable and inexpressible lose their glory when all we have is human language.

Finally, a diagram is offered below to show the relation of space and time images.

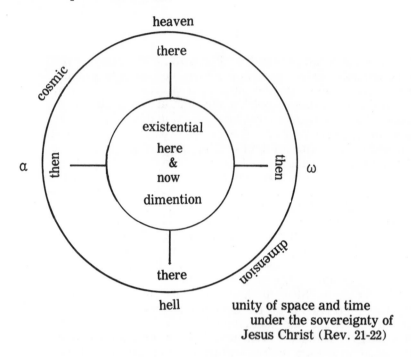

unity of space and time
under the sovereignty of
Jesus Christ (Rev. 21-22)

Eph. 1:9-10

Diagram 14

As shown in the above diagram, the spatial imagery and time imagery can be connected to each other by the Cross of Christ which symbolizes his self-sacrificial saving act. This means that the connection of the space and time dimensions is achieved through the dynamic value making of Christ so that space (the world) and time (history) may have new meaningful quality or value. The spatial language of the highest heaven can be connected with the temporal language of the ever-lasting or eternal life when the trans-spatio and trans-temporal act of Ascension is well understood. Our faith language expresses that Jesus Christ went up and entered his eternal (trans-temporal), heavenly (trans-spatial) light (value) or life (value).

Another connection which the Cross of Christ makes is that of the cosmic-existential dimensions. The cosmic dimension of 'there' and 'then' in which such words as heaven, earth, hell, Alpha or Omega, are used, is connected with the existential dimension of 'here' and 'now' by the unifying act of Christ. Here St Paul's words are meaningful: "For he has made known to us in all wisdom and insight the mystery of his will, according to his purpose which he set forth in Christ as a plan for the fullness of time, *to unite all things* in him, things in heaven and things on earth." (Eph. 1:9-10).

Now we turn to another section to further discuss the Ascension of Christ.

Case Study: Ascension Story (II)

A. Historical Context

Our text here is another Ascension Story shown in the conclusion of Matthean Gospel (Mt. 28:16-20). In discussing this text, some other ascension language, that is, John's, St. Paul's, and Hebrew's ascension stories will be involved.

According to Alan Richardson, who follows C.H. Dodd in form critical analysis of the text, the Ascension story and some post-resurrection appearance stories (ex. Mt.28: 8-10, Jn.20:19-21, etc.) are *pericope* which bear all the characteristics of folk tradition, in which an oft-repeated story is rubbed down and polished, like a water-worn pebble, until noting but the essential remains, in its most arresting and memorable form.[17] R.H. Fuller says that the Matthean Ascension reflects the tradition of evangelical mission carried out by the earliest Christian community. The Matthean phraseology, 'make disciples of nation' indicates the motivation of mission charge. This tradition is also found in the longer ending in Mark, which includes the mission charge 'preach the gospels (16:16). R.H. Fuller says that "the longer ending probably represents the earliest tradition, which Matthew has reworded to suit his own interest."[18]

It appears that the above form-critical analysis and its historical exegesis is convincing. The declaration of authority, the command to baptize with trinitarian formula, the final promise of a permanent presence with his disciples, etc., all these Matthean phrases reflect the mission task of the primitive church. Their *parousia* expectation is also related to the mission motif.

However, a more important thing in the Matthean story is to interpret the text from our spatio-temporal perspective so that it can have significant relevance to our Christian life situation.

The Matthean Ascension is very different from the Lucan writings in presenting the last scene of the risen Christ (Lk. 24:50-53; Acts 1:1-10); The latter presents Jesus Christ as being taken to heaven; the former does not mention this cosmic scene. This suggests that the Matthean text reflects a more primitive tradition, which regarded the resurrection and the ascension as two episodes in the same process.

Whatever textual criticism of this says, our main concern in the Ascension story is its spatio-temporal expressions and hermeneutical meaning. Regardless of the original writer's intention and the situation of the primitive church, the Ascension text has its own semantic right so that the meaning of the text comes to us and meets us meaningfully today. This is also true of other forms of Christ's Resurrection-Ascension, which we can find in the Fourth Gospel (John 20:17, 19, cf.1:14), Pauline writings (Rom 8:34; Phil 2:9, etc.) and Hebrews (Heb. 4:14, 7:3, 16, 23-25, etc.). Insofar as the original author's psychological intentions and the situations of the original readers are concerned, the different traditions of the primitive church are involved, and even if we exhaust the search for this historical-critical information, the real meaning of the text cannot be understood to us. Yet this does not mean that our hermeneutical work may give up the historical-critical study. We still need the scientific research in its proper context, yet not too much. This problem involves the serious theological dispute called 'historical Jesus and

Kerygmatic Christ', which had a heated discussion among the post-Bultmannian scholars and others in the 1960s to 70s. But our point here is enough to admit some basic reality of historical knowledge for interpreting the text. The more important thing is that the meaning of the text becomes semantically independent of historical knowledge such as the author's intention and can mean whatever it means. In this new hermeneutical light, the most important semantic and hermeneutical factor is space and time language, of which the semantic meaning is of universal significance. In other words, the spatio-temporal image language and its semantic meaning is universally effective for communication. Whether the biblical author was conscious of this truth or not, the semantic meaning of the spatio-temporal language has its own communicative power.

B.   Four Semantic Parts and Interpretations: the Indicative, Imperative, Promise and Liturgical Language

1.   *The Indicative Language*

Let us then examine the language of the Matthean text and its semantic structure. The story of Matthean Ascension can be analyzed into four semantic parts: Indicative, imperative, promise and liturgical language. There is no doubt that the story is characterized by spatial and temporal images or picture language. What then are these four parts? By quoting the text, We will indicate their semantic factors: "When they saw him they worshiped him (liturgical); ..... Jesus came and said to them, 'All authority in heaven and on earth has been given to me (indicative). Go therefore and make disciples of all nations, baptizing them in the name of the Father and of the Son and of the Holy Spirit, teaching them to observe all that I

have commanded you (Imperative and liturgical) and lo, I
am with you always to the close of the age (promise)'."

The above four factors in the story are generally applicable to the Exodus-Wilderness, which is the main subject of the Old Testament, and also to other Ascension
stories of the New Testament, in which Christological
meaning finds expression. The indicative language of the
Exodus-Wilderness, in which spatial and temporal images
are dominant factors, includes the series of theophany and
accompanying miracles, which Moses and his people had
experienced. This indicative language is characterized by
God's revealing words and saving acts which find expression in the height image of Mt. Sinai, and the descent image of *Shekhinah,* in the wilderness, in which bright cloud
or smoke is involved. In the biblical sense, the appearance
of bright cloud or smoke means God's coming down to visible presence.   In our spatio-temporal semantics, this
means that trans-spatio and trans-temporal God appears
in the spatio-temporal sphere. This is the main image of
spatio-temporal indicative language in the Exodus-
Wilderness story. This *Shekhinah* theophany imagery is
meaningfully reflected in the Incarnation language in the
fourth Gospel: "The Word became flesh and dwelt among
us, full of grace and truth; we have beheld his glory, glory
as of the only Son from the Father." (John 1:14). When examined closely, this Incarnation language is dominated by
spatial and temporal images, yet also by dynamic terms
as shown in the words, 'become flesh' ($\sigma \acute{\alpha} \rho \xi$
$\dot{\epsilon} \gamma \acute{\epsilon} \nu \epsilon \tau o$), which has more dynamic meaning
than 'descending'. Further attention should be paid to the
expression 'dwelt among us' ($\dot{\epsilon} \sigma \kappa \acute{\eta} \nu \omega \sigma \epsilon \nu \; \dot{\epsilon} \nu$
$\dot{\eta} \mu \widetilde{\iota} \nu$). Here the reflection of *Shekhinah* of
Exodus-Wilderness is apparent. Alan Richardson says
that "The kind of play on words that is beloved of the
Semitic mind can be reproduced in biblical Greek by the
rough assonance of the words *shekhinah,*
$\dot{\epsilon} \pi \iota \sigma \kappa \iota \acute{\alpha} \zeta \epsilon \iota \nu$ (to overshadow) and $\sigma \kappa \eta \nu \acute{\eta}$ (a
tabernacle, tent) or $\sigma \kappa \eta \nu \epsilon \widetilde{\iota} \nu$ (to dwell in a tent,
encamp). Thus, in the Transfiguration story, the cloud
(Mk. 9:7, Lk 9:34; Mt. 17:5, significantly, a *bright* cloud)

represents the cloud which overshadowed the 'tent of meeting' when the glory of Yahweh filled the tabernacle (Ex. 40:34ff), and the same verb, ἐπισκιάζειν is used"[19]

The above paragraphs are to show that the indicative language of Ascension initially includes Incarnation language (or the language of Christ's descending) which finds expression in spatial and temporal words. The Resurrection and Ascension of Christ presuppose his descending and humiliation. This means that, without Incarnation, without God's participation in a space and time situation, his trans-spatio and trans-temporal Exaltation cannot take place in our human knowledge and language. In this sense, the Incarnated Word is the linguistic *logos* for human communication as well as God's saving will and action. In our spatial and temporal semantics the *logos* means not only trans-spatial and trans-temporal reality of God's purpose, but also its spatio-temporal formation. From this it follow that the *kerygmatic* Christ cannot be separable from historic Jesus. In this connection, the words of the first letter of John are meaningful: "We write to you about the Word of life, which has existed from the very beginning: We have heard it, and we have seen it with our eyes ..... when this life became visible, we saw it ..... "(1 John 1:1-2, Good News Bible).

Here some space and time language can be indicated and interpreted for hermeneutical understanding. "

ὁ ὦν ἀπ' ἀρχῆς (That which was from beginning) is linguistic symbolism of the trans-spatial and trans-temporal divine event as pre-existent Word. The word ὦν (existed) does not accompany its spatial relation or locality while indicating its temporal relation ἀπ' ἀρχῆς (from beginning). But the 'beginning' is a symbolic word for an unexpressible trans-temporal meaning, which refers to the beginning of creation. In the Fourth Gospel and in John's writings, Jesus Christ as the pre-existent Word presents his divine character in terms of trans-spatial and trans-temporal Being. The Incarnation or historical Jesus presupposes his trans-spatio and trans-temporal divine status. In this sense, the Matthean and other Ascension stories are extended back to the pre-existent Word.

Now let us to turn to the meaning of Ascension. By Ascension here we mean a semantic process of Christ's Exaltation which includes his resurrection, Ascension and present status at God's right hand. The Ascension of Christ, as the paradoxical vindication of the descended and humiliated historical Jesus, means that the human spatial and temporal situation is deeply redeemed and transformed into a new trans-spatial and trans-temporal dimension by the saving act of Christ. This also means that our new life experience in Christ is a new existence, which is transformed through Christian faith, expressed as looking up to an ascending Christ. Christian living and language here still belong to the spatio-temporal sphere, yet spiritual life and hope are directed to a trans-spatio and trans-temporal dimension. In other words, Christian life is laid across two worlds, a physical world and a spiritual world, a spatio-temporal dimension and a trans-spatio trans-temporal dimension. But this does not mean that the reality of Christian life is dualistic, that is, physical and spiritual, downward and upward or spatio-temporal and trans-spatio trans-temporal. Natural human existence can be regarded as dualistic or directed downwards, in the sense that it follows the more physical way rather than the spiritual life. The religious existence of the Old Testament, as shown in the Exodus-Wilderness situation rather can be interpreted as upward movement, even though the spiritual situation of the ancient Hebrew was frail and tempted to the Egyptian meat pot. The conclusion of the Old Testament story is the eventual crossing of the Jordan River and the victorious occupation of the Promised Land, in spite of many tragic destructions on the way.

Christian existence, or life in Christ, is expressed as positive and dynamic upward movement in the sense that Christians follow the victorious way of Christ, who overcame all kinds of physical or spatial-temporal preventions, even though there are still many temptations and existential tensions between the present and the past, and the present and the future. This is the existential meaning of the Ascension. Yet we have to go further in order to discover the fullness of the meaning of the Ascended Christ.

Christ's Exaltation as the process of resurrection, Ascension and participation in Heavenly power, is not only for personal or existential meaning. Here another dimension of meaning comes in. Our Matthean text of Ascension stresses the meaning of a cosmic dimension when it says that "All authority in heaven and on earth has been given to me." The trans-spatio and trans-temporal triumph of Christ expressed in the Ascension language is not only for the transcendent experience of personal existence, but also for the transformation of the whole world and history into new life dimensions. When we interpret this aspect in terms of value dimension, such value words as light and power are involved because of their symbolic and universal meaning. The light is not only for personal awakening or internal truth, it is also for the whole world and universe, that is, God's creation. Jesus says that "I am the light of the world." Jesus healed particular blind individuals and gave light to them, yet he also wanted to be called a light tower able to throw its light to a far distance. The light has cosmic power to drive out the thick darkness, which is the symbol of sinful world. Here the meaning of light is connected with another value word, that is, the 'power' of Christ. When we say that Christ ascended to heaven and sits at the right hand side of God, it means that Christ shares almighty power with God, which our faith language expresses as sitting at the heavenly throne. His power is of cosmic significance, and drives out all kinds of demonic powers or evil forces. This value word thus has semantic and hermeneutical relevance to us. The continuing serious problem of life is of evil forces which darkens our personal and social existence. Without solving this problem, there is no hope and salvation. The triumphant language of the Ascended Christ is about his power over evil forces. This evil power belongs to the spatio-temporal sphere. Thus, to possess all mighty power over the spatial-temporal powers, Christ must ascend to heaven beyond the spatio-temporal category. The Ascended Christ has heavenly divine power and exercises it as a cosmic Ruler and judge. This image comes from the language of the Book of Revelation.

The above statements emphasize the ontological meaning of trans-spatio and trans-temporal power. Our human life needs not only personal or existential life power, but also trans-spatial and trans-temporal ontological power. This also means that our human life demands the revealing dimension of transcendent power. The Giver of the Power is Christ, who ascended to heaven.

2) *The Imperative Language*

Now we turn to the next part of the Matthean Ascension, that is, the imperative language. The bridge word between the indicative and the imperative is always the conjunction, *therefore* (οὖν). Matthew says "Go therefore and make disciples of all nations ....."
(πορευθέντες οὖν μαθητεύσατε πάντα
    τὰ ἔθνη).

The structure of the indicative-imperative is characteristic of the Pauline Epistles. God's revealing grace and his saving act in Christ demand our active response. On our part, the indicative-imperative scheme means that our faith cannot be separable from ethical obligations. In this context, Jesus's words are particularly important: "As I have loved you, you also have to love your brothers." St. James stresses this imperative when he says, "What does it profit, my brethren, if a man says, he has faith but no works? ... so faith by itself, if it has no works, is dead" (James 2:14, 17). the First Letter of John also emphasizes the scheme of the indicative - imperative in terms of love: "Dear friends, if this is how God loved us (indicative language), then (καὶ), we must (

ὀφεἱλομεν) love one another. (1 John 4:11). "This is, then, is the command (ἐντολὴν   ) that Christ gave us: he who loves God must love his brother also." (καὶ ταύτην τὴν ἐντολὴν ἔχομεν ἀπ᾽αὐτοῦ, ἵνα· ὁ ἀγαπῶν τὸν Θεὸν ἀγαπᾷ καὶ τὸν ἀδελφὸν αὐτοῦ) (I John, 4:21).

The main parts of the Old Testament, that is, the Exodus-Wilderness and the prophetic writings are characterized by the indicative-imperative scheme. They declare God's self-revelation and his saving act, and this indicative language is followed by god's ethical command. In this sense the words, 'Mt. Sinai' has significant connotations. When we say the word, it implies God's theophany (shekhinah) and his Ten Commandments. Theophany language (indicative) is not separable from the Decalogue; God is not an abstract meta-physical reality. The biblical God of Judeo-Christian tradition has been described as the God who came down and spoke of concrete historical situations and acted as the deliverer as shown in the Exodus story. But the more important thing is to know that the merciful and acting God demands active response from his people. Jesus Christ who declared the coming of heavenly kingdom also demands his disciples to obey his new commandment of love. His indicative language is not separable from his imperative commandment of love. This ethical imperative is the intrinsic part of the Gospels and constitutes the kerygma itself.

The semantic and hermeneutical meaning of the imperative language should be found in the value and qualitative dimensions of human inter-relationships. Our human social experiences give us the importance of constructive human relationships which accompanies positive value consciousness. This value consciousness might begin with the primitive group experiences of Homo sapiens in which the instinctive and selfish behaviours were proved destructive to their group survival. Whatever the origin of the value consciousness is, the important thing is that the value dimension of human life is the product of social life, and has a dichotomous character: hatred and love, dishonesty and honesty, impatience and patience, ugliness and beauty, unforgiveness and forgiveness, and so on. In this sense the beautiful story of the Garden of Eden implies that behind the writing of the story, there was an ugly and terrible human situation. The primary experiences of human social relations have been often negative ones, which we still experience today. However, the dark side of social experience has been always corrected or changed by the human transcendent spirit, and knowledge which human science, arts, literary works, moral teachings or religions have contributed in the human history and culture. Here value words are formed, taught and transmitted to next generations. There are, of course, many distortions of value words and abuses, yet our society and culture still inspires us with affirmative meanings of such value words as kindness, love, help, encouragement, sharing, community spirit, justice, and peace. These are all linguistic forms of the qualitative dimension of human life. The understanding of these value words is not the mere acknowledgement of the qualitative dimension, but indicates active personal participation. For this reason, the value words often have connections with imperative language. Particularly religious teaching and Christian language stress the ethical imperative.

Human existence is basically ethical existence. Here Erich Fromm's words are worthy to note: 'In the process of living, man relates himself to the world (1) by acquiring and assimilating things, and (2) by relating himself to people (and himself). The former I shall call the process of assimilation; the latter, that of socialization. Both forms of relatedness are 'open' and not, as with the animal, instinctively determined.''[20] This social and transcendental character of human existence implies the ethical dimension of responsibility and response. Again, Fromm says that "Responsibility is not a duty imposed upon one from the outside, but is my response to a request which I feel to be my concern. Responsibility and response have the same root, *respondere* = 'to answer'; to be responsible means to be ready to respond.''[21]

Fromm's ethical psychology has further dynamic significance when he emphasizes on the ethic of love: "To love one person productively means to be related to human core, to him as representing mankind, ... All men are in need of help and depend on one another."[22]

We also agree with the power of dynamic dimension of an ethical imperative, which Fromm stresses in his psychoanalysis, which is distinct from Freudian *libido* organization. Fromm puts emphasis on the ability of man to make productive use of his power, and writes that "With his power of reason he can penetrate the surface of phenomena and understand their essence. With his power of love he can break through the wall which separate one person from another. With his power of imagination he can visualize things not yet existing."[23]

However, Fromm's ethical power of man should not be a pantheistic entity. We believe that the ethical nature of the human person can be explicated and powerful only when it is seen in the light of God's revealing dimension, which we understand in indicative language. Without this indicative language, the ethical teaching of human relationships is weak and implicit. The horizontal dimension of human brotherly love should not be separated from the vertical dimension of God's Love. Here is the reason why the Christ's imperative words are spoken in the context of the Ascension story.

3. *The Promise Language*

The next part of the Matthean Ascension is about the Promise language. The meaning of promise language is different from that of the indicative or imperative language. The promise belongs to a future category, yet it stresses assurance. In the Ascension story of the Acts of the Apostles, the promise is expressed in terms of a futuristic *parousia* when it says that "This Jesus, who was taken up from you into heaven, will come back in the same way that you saw him go to heaven."(Acts 1:11).

The Matthean Gospel also includes the futuristic coming of Jesus Christ, particularly when it talks about the parables of heavenly kingdom or the Final Judgement (Mt. Ch.24). Yet, the promise in the Matthean Ascension stresses the immanent spiritual presence of Ascended Christ: "I will be with you always, to the end of the age" (MT. 28:29). This promise should be understood in connection with the coming and presence of the Holy Spirit.

The promissory element of biblical language has historical importance for biblical faith. The terms the Old Testament and New Testament, or the Old Covenant and New Covenant themselves imply promise. We know that the books of the Old Testament are rich in promissory words. God's promises made to Abraham, Moses, David and many others, are assurances recorded in the Old Testament. The Promised Land, the idea of a remnant, the Messianic prophecy, and Joel's prophecy concerning the outpouring of the Spirit of God, all these belong to the Old Testament promise. This is even more true of the New Testament language. The Parables of the Kingdom of God, the *parousia* language, the sending of *Paraclete* (παράκλητος) and Apocalyptic prophecy are New Testament promise terms. The Epistle to the Hebrews also expresses the meaning of the promise in spatio-temporal terms:

> They did not receive the things God had promised, but for a long way off they saw and welcomed them, and admitted openly that they were foreigners and refugees on earth. Those who say such things make it clear that they are looking for a country of their own.
> They did not think back to the country they had left; if they had, they would have had the chance to return.
> Instead, it was a better country they longed for, the heavenly country. And so God is not ashamed to have them call him their God, for he has prepared a city for them (Heb.11:13-16).

St. Paul expresses the meaning of the promise in terms of a prize or the crown of righteousness which the Lord will give on that day (Phil. 3:14, 2 Tim. 4:8, etc.). For St. Paul, the prize or Crown which God promised is the most important goal to achieve.

Now let us consider the semantic and hermeneutical meaning of promise language. Whatever the different biblical texts refer to in their historical contexts, the ultimate meaning of the promise language is existential and ontological. By 'existential' we mean personal and internal dimension, and by 'ontological' we mean transcendent divine reality. Professor Macquarrie interprets the concept of hope in terms of human freedom and the dynamics of action. He writes that "hope belongs essentially to any truly personal existence. Where freedom is denied, whether in practical terms through oppression or in theoretical terms through some deterministic ideology, hope is denied also; and where hope is denied, persons are being destroyed, for to be a person means, among other things, to be constantly projecting oneself in hope toward goals in which personal being will find fuller expression and satisfaction."[24] In regard to the dynamic dimension of hope, Macquarrie quotes St. Thomas Aquinas' words as the true dynamic of human striving and patience: "Hope's object is a good that lies in the future and that is difficult but possible to attain."[25]

The above quotations show the existential and dynamic meaning of hope. But the hope is not strong enough to stand all kinds of spatial and temporal finitudes, and negative reality including sinful situations, sufferings and death, even though hope's dynamic character is recognized and proved in our practical life experience. This means that human hope should be confirmed and transformed by the assurance which trans-spatial and trans-temporal Being gives to his people under the name of promise. The permanently trusted promise is not possible at the human level. God is the only guarantor of promise who is beyond spatial and temporal boundaries. This does not mean that our human hope and human promise are untrustful and meaningless ones. In our personal life and social slogans, there are certain degrees of trustfulness and reliability. It is true that, without religious goal or faith, human beings struggle for their ideals, and in some cases, men even sacrifice their lives for their countries or justice causes. However, our history and experience teach us that, without religiously assured hope or faith, our life is just like the ancient Hebrews, who were wandering about in the wilderness. Conversely this means that human life is meaningful and powerful when ultimate goals or purposes are set through religious faith. Of course, we admit that there have been many serious mistakes and corruptions in historical religious teachings and life. However, genuine hope and reliability are still to be found in religious faith and life rightly interpreted and understood.

Here is the reason why the promise language of the Matthean and other New Testament ascension stories is of great importance to our faith and life. The divine promise of the victorious Ascension gives Christian people another value of life goal and power which can be universally communicated in inspired human beings. The genuine and authoritative promise has a transcendent dimension, as expressed in the Ascension, in which Christ gives a divine promise to those disciples who were looking up him.

4. The Liturgical Language of the Ascension

Finally, we should note that the Matthean and other Ascension stories in the New Testament are closely related to liturgical language. The Matthean text says that "When they saw him they worshiped him." (Mt. 28:17) The mention of baptism, in the Trinitarian formula, also suggests that the Ascension story was formed against the liturgical background of the primitive church. This may be clearer when we examine the Lucan Ascension, written in the last chapter of the Gospel (Lk 24:50-53). In this passage the words or phrases like 'raised his hands' 'blessed them' 'worshipped him' 'filled with great joy' 'spent all their time in the Temple giving thanks to God', all these reflect the liturgical language of the primitive church. The liturgical imageries shown in the Epistle to Hebrews and in the Revelation to John further confirm the liturgical use of the Ascension story.[26]

Let us then consider the semantic and hermeneutical meaning of the liturgical language. In the religious world and its history, there have been many different types of liturgical expressions. This is also true of the Christian world and history. The history of Christian liturgy includes many different liturgical traditions. However, I wonder how many books have been devoted to search into the Christian liturgy from a spatio-temporal and value perspective. Our examination of the biblical language, particularly Ascension language, emphasizes its liturgical background, which, in turn, is closely related to an evangelical mission motif.

Here we should ask why the liturgical language is closely connected with the ascension stories, with their space and time imageries. In order to answer this question, let us begin with the value dimension of liturgy or worship.

The word *worship* comes from an Anglo-Saxon word *worth ship*, to place a value upon. The affirmative and universal core factor of human personal and communal life is value, or the qualitative experience of life. This dimension may be clearer when we watch its negative forms like hatred, despair, painfulness, ugliness, falsehood or darkness. Love, hope, beauty, joy, truth or light are the affirmative values, which are further valued by such spatial and temporal images as 'height', 'highest place' or 'ever-lasting.' The value dimension is connected with symbolism of a transcendent God, who is addressed as the Holy God or almighty God. In this sense, the worship or liturgy can be called the sanctification of life and action. Our human life finds expression in worship as a value formation. But here we should be careful not to use the phrase, 'the sanctification of life' as a pantheistic concept, which was widespread in ancient world and modern primitive trivial societies.

Christian worship or liturgy is interpreted and understood in Christian faith in God who is the creator of the universe and man. In this connection, the indicative words of the Matthean Ascension, "I have been given all authority in heaven and on earth," is of liturgical significance.

The next thing to note in interpreting the liturgical language is its spatio-temporal relation. Further discussion of this will be found in the last part of the present study. Our point here is that Christian worship or liturgy sanctifies the meaning of spatio-temporal language and life. Here, M. Eliade's terms, the sanctification of time and the sanctification of space, are worthy to note.[27]

However, the more important thing here is to discover the semantic and hermeneutical meaning of the liturgical words of the biblical text. When we read the words, 'heaven' and 'earth' 'always' or 'the end of the age' in the Christological faith, their intuitive semantic meaning is detached from its primary sense and context, and meet us at the depth of our spatio-temporal existence, arousing our value consciousness, and inspiring us to look up and worship the ascended Christ, who overcame all kinds of spatio-temporal boundaries and transforming them meaningfully.

The space and time language of the Bible starts with the image or symbolism of Paradise, which was lost, and concludes it with another image of Paradise regained through the redemptive act of Jesus Christ, who sacrificed himself on the cross according to God's will. The story of Paradise lost and regained means that human being ultimately seeks for trans-spatial and trans-temporal Reality, which is expressed as the heavenly eternal home where there is no longer spatio-temporal suffering and finitude. But our pilgrimage to the heavenly eternal home still takes place in this spatio-temporal sphere through imperative words.

PART III: INTEGRATIVE CONCLUSION

In this final part, we will assess and conclude the subject matter of this hermeneutic study, which has been critically presented and interpreted in the above two parts, in an experimental perspective as a Christian preacher and teacher. Thus, the present study of the space and time language in the New Testament will have further significance relating to author's personal and professional effectiveness.

Chapter VIII

God-Language and
Its Hermeneutical Application

1. *Theology and People's Living Language*

Theology itself, as an intellectual clarification and interpretation of faith, cannot be isolated from the whole life of the church, which includes community faith, worship and action. Traditionally, the faith of the church has been understood as belief or intellectual assent, and its doctrinal theology has frequently been of an abstract and academic kind. But theology is not an intellectual game that can be pursued on its own, but part of a much bigger whole. Theology makes sense only in the context of the

In this connection, it is interesting and important to recognize the dynamic aspect of the word 'theology'. The 'theology' as God-word or God-language (θεός – λόγος) includes not only the scientific sense of the specific study but also its dynamic meaning. According to Ludwig Wittgenstein, ''the speaking of ing. According to Ludwig Wittgenstein, ''the speaking of language is part of an activity, or of a form of life.''[1] This is particularly true of theological language which explicates the meaning of God's revealing act and of the faith-life response of Christian people. This dynamic aspect of Christian theology is meaningfully understood and experienced by parish or local preachers who live in the midst of their people and communicate in their living language. By the living language here, we mean the expressions of total life of the people including their grief, joy, hope, action and all life experiences. This means that the Christian preacher is the participant of people's thinking, feeling and will, which are of their constituent. In this sense, we believe that theology should be a hermeneutic work through which the biblical and theological language can be interpreted meaningfully and powerfully in the context of people's living faith and language.

One of the serious problems the church faces today is that there is a big gap between traditional theological teachings and people's living language. There are still many parish preachers who do not know what the theological hermeneutics means. In many cases, when a preacher is not conscious of or neglects his hermeneutic task, he merely becomes part of his congregation. He might be busy with many other things like administrative works, visitations or program activities etc., but this does not mean that he is a successful minister or preacher. The primary task of a parish preacher is to preach or proclaim God's message to his people. But this task is not simple. Here two questions can be raised: What is God's message? How can we preach the message meaningfully and powerfully? The former is the question of clarifying the *kerygma*, and the latter is the methodological question of interpreting and communicating the kerygmatic language. The *kerygmatic* message, the Church's saving proclamation, has been well known since C. H. Dodd's *The Apostolic Preaching* and other scholarly works. Yet the question of how to preach the kerygma, that is, the hermeneutic question remains unsolved. The reason for this is that the hermeneutic question involves people's living language and the local preacher's hermeneutic task. The Christian preacher or minister has to be conscious of the hermeneutic problem and task. Otherwise, his function as the interpreter and communicator of God's message cannot be properly carried out. When this hermeneutic function and task of the preacher is not carried out or distorted, his church becomes an institutional organization which repeats or stresses its traditional doctrines and practice without any criticism. If such a situation grows worse through the church in general, its religion and society are corrupt and distorted.

The typical example of such a situation can be found in the Pharisaic religion of Jesus' time. The Pharisaic leaders' and teachers' way of teaching their Scripture, which is the Mosaic Law, was literal and legalistic, and their life was hypocritical. These ways of teaching and life were criticized by Jesus, who introduced his new way of teaching and new life. The writer of St. Mark's Gospel says that "The people who heard him were amazed at the way he taught. He wasn't like the teachers of the Law; instead, he taught with authority." (Mark 1:22). For example, when he was asked about a divorce notice, Jesus interprets the matter as follows: "Moses wrote this commandment for you because you are so hard to teach. But in the beginning, at the time of creation, it was said, 'God made them male and female .... and the two will become one. So they are no longer two, but one. Man must not separate, then, what God has joined together." (Mark 10:5-9). Jesus' way of biblical interpretation, that is, his hermeneutic principle comes from his keen insight into the depth of human total existence and his faith in the Divine love. He interprets the meaning of the Sabbath in terms of 'the good of man': "The Sabbath was made for the good of man; man was not made for the Sabbath." (Mark 2:27). In this connection, I can say something about R. Bultmann's contribution. Insofar as his criticism of literal and mythical understanding of the biblical language, Bultmann's existential and anthropological interpretation can be justified. Unless it is accepted in exclusive terms, there is a substantial reality in his interpretation. His hermeneutic contribution, I think, is that he discovered the real problem for church today, one of which theologians and church leaders were not or insufficiently aware in the past Christian centuries and even today.

This author can attest to this through his personal experiences. When I became a Christian member in Korea,

at the age of over twenty and paid attention to the
language of our local preacher and people in the church,
my first awareness was that their language was of a quite
old fashioned kind. Later, when I had more experience of
the church, I realized why their language had been different and less communicable than public modern
language of society. There were, it seemed to me, two
reasons: one was because those Christian people had their
religious experiences in a faith community in which such a
different style of language has developed; the other was
because of their poor communication skills and conser-
vatism. The former might be understood in terms of a
special character of religious talk, but the latter was the
problem. They were keeping a very old fashioned and
poorly translated Bible, and got used to such an old
language. This was the problem, yet they did not or did not
want to realize the problem. The preacher and people of
the church were very conservative and their knowledge of
the Bible was of a literal and fundamentalistic kind.

I think that this type of literalism is not so far from
that of the Pharisaic religion. I have had opportunities to
study at progressive theological institutes where my interest in the religious communication problem has been
explored and considered in more explicit terms. In this
process of my theological thought, I found that one of
Bultmann's great contributions was his discovery of the
real problem for church today and his hermeneutic attempt to solve the problem. His hermeneutic approach is
existential and anthropological. Unless it is accepted in
exclusive terms, his existential and anthropological interpretation helps us to understand one of the hermeneutic
aspects which Jesus shows us in his biblical interpretation.
As I already mentioned, Jesus had a keen insight into the
depth of human heart and life, and accordingly, his way of
interpreting the Scripture is anthropological.

Now we have to come back to another aspect of Jesus'
new teaching, that is, his hermeneutic language. As we
know, Jesus' words and language are an ordinary and living language like bread, water, friend, bird, sheep and

goats, labourers in the vineyard, soils and sower and etc. He used ordinary words, but in many cases applied them in special settings, so that a special meaning could be expressed. For instance, Jesus said that he was the light, but the light of the world. He said that he was the bread but the bread of life. The kingdom of heaven, the coming of the Son of Man, the prodigal son and his father's love, etc., all these are his hermeneutic language which is easily understood by ordinary people, yet which gives them special meaning. We call this type of language image or symbolic language. Yet Jesus' symbolic language is of a cognitive kind. Then, how about our sermons and hermeneutic language? Many preachers or ministers in the church today are not conscious of the importance of the function of language. Especially when they are interested in an academic concept and terminology, their homiletic language easily becomes abstract while losing the sensuous, imagery and concrete expressions. We acknowledge that, for some intellectually trained people, a philosophical or conceptual type of sermon is necessary rather than the sensuous and ordinary language. However, most of Christian members in the church need the daily sensuous language which can be communicated to them. Here we can point out Bultmann's mistake which was made in his light treatment of symbolic language. Bultmann's anti-symbolic position comes from protestant subjectivism in which God's presence and approach to man are understood almost exclusively in terms of the word of preaching. The Protestantism puts stress on preaching, instruction, hearing, understanding, that is to say, on what goes on in our mind. Professor Maquarrie calls this type of thinking intellectualism or conceptualism, which includes docetism.[2]

2.   *Liturgical Spatio-Temporal Language and*
      Preacher's Hermeneutic Task

In this connection, I would like to stress the meaning of
Christian worship in which I participates as a
celebrant. Christian worship is our active response, faith-
life response, to God's revealing action and saving grace.
This faith-life response is to be expressed through our
liturgical language, that is, confessional, praising and
adoring language which are made of the value and quality
to our life.   Our knowledge of God and its theological
language is not a pure intellectual or a conceptual assent
to the Divine truth; it is completed through our shared experiences and incorporation.   Man is an embodied
creature of flesh and blood, and Christianity is the religion
of Incarnation. This means that our true knowledge of God
comes through our senses as well as through our minds.
The purpose of our Christian worship, especially of the
sacramental liturgy is not so much instruction as incorporation.   This in turn fights against the individualistic
subjectivism and abstract docetism, and teaches appreciation for the ontological divine reality.
      We believe that the meaning of Christian worship as
the active response of faith-life is grounded on Jesus'
teaching and life. His saving message about the kingdom
of God is not a mere verbal announcement.   His judgement, behaviour, action and life are also his hermeneutic
language of the saving message.   He not only taught the
kingdom of God, he also showed it through his behaviour,
love and self-sacrificial action.   In this sense, his crucifixion was the hermeneutic decision and action.   Our Christian worship is inseparable from the behavioural
language. Worship or liturgy means the service of God,
and this in turn implies loving and delivering our
neighbour.   Our true knowledge of God is possible only
when we participate and experience these loving activities.   This also means that our true theological
knowledge should come from our practical loving actions

and experiences. The writer of the First Letter of John says, "Dear friends, let us love one another, for love comes from God. Whoever loves is a child of God and knows God. Whoever does not love does not know God, because God is love." (I John 4:7-8). Our Christian worship, especially our sacramental liturgy, including Holy Eucharist, is the way of experiencing the presence of God through hearing and seeing God's saving act in Jesus Christ. Worship is also the way of responding to the saving act through our liturgical language and expressions.   The liturgical language is that of adoration or confession, which includes linguistic acts.   When it is said in a funeral oration 'We mourn our ...' this is surely supposed to be an expression of mourning; not to tell anything to those who are present. In the same way, 'We are truly sorry and repent' constitutes an *act* of repentance, not the communication of information.   Liturgical language bids the worshipper engage in *acts* : in pledge, in pardonings, in promises, in guarantees in acceptance, in acts of repentance, and in acts of worship.

In the above paragraph, we discussed the active character of worship and liturgical language. This is to say that our true knowledge of God and theological language should be completed in the liturgical context. This is also true in our knowledge of the New Testament *kerygma*, which is the key message in the early church. It is believed that, without understanding its liturgical setting in the early church, the meaning of the *kerygma* cannot be appropriately interpreted, because the message of the early church is expressed in liturgical language and context. The New Testament is rich in liturgical language, including baptismal and sacrificial language. The narration of Christ's birth and ascension story are also to be interpreted in the liturgical context.

As a celebrant and interpreter, the priest or minister of the church has to know about and participate in what he is doing in the liturgical activity and language. His sermon, liturgical service and life are all hermeneutic efforts to give further contributions to the theological language and practical life of the church.

Now we will turn to the space and time language which is the specific subject of the present study. We will interpret the meaning of the space and time language in the author's personal and community faith and language which reflects his experimental context. Before examining the topic, I would like to mention some personal experience.

Since my early teens, I have had a question about endless space and time. My increased knowledge of the scientific world has given me some information about the universe in terms of unlimited space and time, but it could not give an answer to my deep, mysterious questioning. Since I became a Christian in my early twenties and then studied theology, I found that the implicit question I have had was an existential kind of question which could not be answered by any scientific or objective information. This explicit awareness of the personal and existential knowledge came from my study of Bultmann's theology, particularly of his theological hermeneutics. Bultmann has helped me to have an insight into the anthropological and existential meaning of the New Testament mythology, which includes space and time language. He rejects any objectified meaning of the space and time expressions. When his rejection is directed to fundamentalist faith, which believes literally the space and time language like 'God is in heaven', and to its opposite extreme faith, liberal faith which rejects any mythological or symbolical expressions as meaningless illusions, Bultmann's critical position is right and meaningful, but in the church even today, there are still many people who have just such a fundamental faith or liberal type of faith without any critical notion of their faith. These two extreme types of faith and their theological assertions have caused many troubles, and asserted negative influences on our Christian faith and life. Whenever I teach or talk to such people, I have realized how important it is for me to know and use Bultmann's existential interpretation of mythological language.

However, the pendulum has swung the other way. As we already discussed in the previous chapters, Bultmann's

over emphasis on anthropological and existential interpretation of the New Testament mythological language,
especially of its spatial and temporal language, resulted
not only in de-mythologizing, but also in de-symbolizing of
the language. This is another danger to Christian faith and
life. The Christian church has kept various kinds of symbolic expressions, verbal or non-verbal. We admit that
there have been many misuses or superstitious uses of
symbolic language. In spite of all these mistakes and
dangers, the church still needs the symbolic form and
meaning of the religious language. This assertion can be
supported by a tendency in the evangelical Protestant
churches in the past decades. In the Protestant churches,
there have been increased desires for liturgical worship
and symbolism. More Protestant ministers became interested in the liturgical calendar, liturgical preaching,
Eucharistic service, altar, candle light and even the
clerical collar. These are all symbolic forms of religious
and faith reality, yet in many cases, they are taken or applied to their services and life without adequate knowledge
of their symbolic function and meaning. The symbolic
forms and meanings are useful and meaningful only when
they are appropriately interpreted and communicated intelligibly to the participants.

Here we come back to our specific subject, the symbolic language of space and time. I believe that the most
significant and powerful symbolism of religious language
is to be found in the space and time language. Our Christian Bible and church are rich in spatio-temporal expressions. As space and time language in the Bible has been
dealt with, here we will talk about its liturgical expressions in our church and its meaning.

Space and time expressions in the Christian worship is
a highly symbolized liturgical language, which means the
height and depth of spirituality and its eternal quality. The
space and time language of spirituality is expressed in
credal terms, Psalms or the Hymns, the Doxology, the
Lord's   Prayer, People's   prayers,   the   Offering,
Eucharistic language and all other liturgical expressions.

In liturgical space and time language, our unworthiness is
confessed and the Divine worthiness is praised and adored
in terms of His 'height' and 'eternity'. This is the meaning
of *worship* (worth-ship). The Hebrew liturgical Psalm
writer says:

To you alone, O, Lord, to you alone,
and not to us, must glory be given
because of your constant love and
    faithfulness
        ....

Where is your God?
Our God is in heaven
        ....

We, the living, will give thanks to him
    now and forever. (Psalm 115)

The words of 'O Gracious Light' (*Phos Hilaron*) which
is included in the Evening Prayer of Anglican tradition is
also meaningful in its emotive and worthiness sense and in
its spatio-temporal context. It says:

O gracious Light,
pure brightness of the everliving Father
    in heaven
O Jesus Christ, Holy and blessed
        ....

You are worthy at all times to be
    praised by happy voices,
O Son of God, O Giver of life,
and to be glorified through all worlds.
        (pp. 66-67, B.A.S. The Anglican
        Church of Canada)

Our Christian faith in the Incarnation has its point
solely on the Hebraic presupposition of the otherness, the

transcendence of God. It is because God is infinitely above the world that His coming down into the world is wonderful. What gives the whole meaning to the Christian recognition of God in Christ is that this is the same God before whom man's proper attitude is that of Job's adoration and confession of his own utter unworthiness.

Our natural reaction to the revelation of some supreme beauty in man or nature is the impulse to bow down before it. This is even more the case when we are struck with a mysterious Divine awe or a spiritual experience. No one can say that this is an unworthy self-abasement. It is the right recognition of consummate worth. It is not accidental that, in early expressions of Christian worship, this note is prominent, "Thou are worthy O Lord, to receive glory and honour and power" (Rev. 4:11).

The *Sanctus,* the hymn of adoration which follows the Preface in the Eucharist also includes its spatio-temporal words in the context of quality and worthiness, so that God's transcendence and his coming are praised and adored.

> Holy, holy, holy,
> God of power and might,
> heaven and earth are full of your glory.
> Hosanna in the highest.
>
> Blessed is he who comes in the name of
> the Lord.
> Hosanna in the highest.

The most valuable and qualitative symbolism of liturgical spatio-temporal language is also found in the doxology and the Lord's Prayer. "Glory to God in the highest, and peace to his people on earth. ..." (the Greater Doxology: the *Gloria in Excelsis*). "Glory to the Father, and to the Son, and to the Holy spirit: as it was in the beginning, is now, and will be for ever. Amen." (the Lesser Doxology: *Gloria Patri*). "Our Father in heaven, hallowed be your name ..." (the Lord's Prayer).

As shown in the above quotations, our liturgical worship is rich in space and time language together with qualitative words like 'glory', 'power', 'holy', 'love', 'blessed', 'worthy', 'praised', and so on. When the space and time language is used with such qualitative words in the liturgical context, its symbolic meaning reaches the highest point of spirituality. No one thinks that the worshippers who read or sing the spacetime language believe those expressions as literal truth. The words, 'heaven', 'high', 'for ever and ever', are symbolic expressions as well as the language of our physical experience. These symbolic words are further symbolized spiritually in their liturgical and qualitative context. The height and length of our spirituality are to be praised and adored with joy, happiness, shouting or the feelings of holiness or worthiness.

However, our liturgical spatio-temporal language is not confined to the emotive language of the praise and glory. Here we turn to the symbolism and meaning of Eucharist, in which the meaning of sacrifice and presence is involved. As Professor Maquarrie indicates rightly, the Holy Eucharist sums up in itself Christian worship, experience, and theology in an amazing richness. It includes all important subjects of Christian theology and life. It combines Word and Sacrament; its appeal is to spirit and sense; it brings together the Calvary and the presence of the risen Christ. It also covers the doctrine of creation, the doctrine of atonement, the doctrine of Incarnation, the meaning of the church, and so on.[3] However, more important meaning of the eucharistic sacrifice and presence is discovered in its spatio-temporal relations.

Let us begin with the eucharistic sacrifice. It is a representing of Christ's saving work, of his self-giving act. In this sense the eucharistic sacrifice has a new meaning in terms of atonement different from the Jewish Temple sacrifice. The new means of the atonement is proclaimed and represented as the gift of God to man. Christ's coming to us and his self-giving on the cross for man's sin and his entrance into the eternal priesthood in heaven are all God's atoning and redemptive act. When the meaning of eucharistic sacrifice is interpreted in this action context, a spatial language is involved. However, here by spatial language, we mean a dynamic and qualitative form of the language we term as an action language. Spatial language is not confined to a place, spot, station or locality which has a static meaning. Our human language is more meaningful and powerful when it is transformed or developed to dynamic form than when left static. In this sense, verbs such as 'come,' 'go,' 'visit,' 'depart,' 'arrive,' 'enter,' or 'fly' are more existential and dynamic than the common referring nouns such as 'tree,' 'mountain,' 'cat,' 'miles,' 'earth,' or 'stars.' We are not static in our biological existence. We human beings are always moving, doing something, and acting. Accordingly, our language has verbs as its dominating factor, which determine or qualify the meaning of the language in its context. In this sense, all kinds of verbs which include the sense of moving, doing and acting are spatial language of another level.

When this action language is applied to religious language, especially to the eucharistic sacrifice of Christian worship, it has a highly symbolized meaning. Here some biblical quotations are needed to understand the spatial active language of Christ's redemption. The writer of the Epistle to the Hebrews, who teaches us about the meaning of Christological worship and sacrifice, says, "Christ entered not into a holy place made with hands, like in pattern to the true; but into heaven itself, now to appear before the face of God for us" (Heb. 9:24). In dealing with the sacrificial or atoning soteriology of the Christ event, the writer of the Epistle uses the symbolic image of the way to heaven, from which Christ came down, sacrificed himself on the earth and ascended to heaven. This image is also applied to his people who are to follow their pioneering savior, Jesus Christ. These Christian people are described as travellers to heavenly home. The writer of the Epistle says, "Having, therefore, brethren, boldness to enter into the holy place, by which he means the Holy of Holies" by the blood of Jesus, by the way which he dedicated for us, ... (Heb. 10:19 ff.).

The above quotations show that the redemptive or atoning sacrifice of the Christ event demands spatial language which symbolizes its spiritual meaning. This shows that Christ, eternal sonship, came down and experienced our human situation of spatial existence and ascended to the heavenly place to open the new way to be followed by his Christian people. This spatial symbolism means that he overcame the finitude of our spatial existence by his self-sacrificial act. Our spatial existence is characterized by sinfulness, anxiety, loneliness, alienation, and a longing for truth and eternity. Jesus Christ, who is the pioneer of the new way to heavenly place, overcame all those situations and ascended into heaven. Here the spatial language "He ascended into heaven" is a liturgical language which acclaims Christ's kingship as shown in Psalm 110:1. The upward spatial language of Christ's sovereignty in its liturgical context means that He is our God who has trans-spatial 'Height' and power. This also means that we Christians, as his followers, are those who believe and participate in the trans-spatial height and power dimension, which is symbolized as 'heaven' or 'heavenly glory'. The writer of the Epistle to the Hebrews stresses that the heavenly and eternal enthronement of Christ came from his historical sacrifice or atonement which culminated on his cross.

The above spatial language and meaning of Eucharistic sacrice brings me to a related question of the Eucharistic presence. In the past decades, there have been some understandings of Eucharistic presence in terms of spatial, temporal or personal dimensions.[4] My discussion here is of its temporal context and meaning.

The Christian Eucharist, which includes the spatial language about the Christ event, also includes the temporal language as a main symbolism. As the liturgical, spatial language is spiritualized in terms of trans-spatial heaven or the sanctified place of the most high, the temporal language in the liturgical context is also spiritualized in terms of trans-temporal eternity, or the sanctified time of 'for ever and ever.' The writer of the Book of the

Revelation says, "Then I saw a new heaven and a new earth. The first heaven and the first earth disappeared, and the sea vanished. And I saw the Holy City, the new Jerusalem, coming down out of heaven from God, ... There will be no more death, no more grief, crying, or pain. The old things have disappeared." (Rev. 21:1-4). This trans-spatial language is followed by the trans-temporal language when the writer says, "It is done! I am the *Alpha* and the *Omega*, the beginning and the end." (Rev. 21:6). These spatial and temporal statements are connected with liturgical terms which urge the serious decision and responsibility of the present life: "Worship God!". ... "Listen!" says Jesus. "I am coming soon! I will bring my rewards with me to give to each one according to what he has done. ... Happy are those who wash their robes clean, and so have the right to eat the fruit from the tree of life, and to go through the gates into the city." (Rev. 22:9, 12-14).

The meaning of our Christian worship, particularly of the Eucharist, is to participate in and experience the temporal and trans-temporal meaning of Christ's event, as well as its spatial and trans-spatial meaning together with its ethical imperatives. The saving act of Jesus Christ is once and for all the eschatological event which took place in a particular place and in a particular time. Nevertheless, this past event has a relevant meaning and effectiveness to our faith and life today when we remember his sacrificial atonement of body and blood, which is symbolized in terms of the consecrated bread and wine, and anticipates the heavenly banquet. The remembrance of the past event and the anticipation of the futuristic completion, are experienced spiritually at the present moment. The theological ground of this eucharistic temporal language can be found in the New Testament, especially in the Epistle to the Hebrews where the liturgical language of Christ's event is interpreted in an eschatological context.

The writer of the Epistle says that "Christ has now appeared once and for all, when all ages of time are nearing the end, to remove sin through the sacrifice of himself"

(Heb. 9:26). Accordingly, this means that Christian people "tasted heaven's gift and received their share of the Holy Spirit. ... They know from experience that God's word is good, and they had felt the powers of the coming age." (Heb. 6:4-5). Nevertheless, our spiritual eyes are directed to the future when our goal will be accomplished. Christians already experienced God's redemptive act in Christ, yet they wait for final completeness. This means that we Christians are situated between the past and the future, or between the two temporal adverbs, 'already' and 'not yet'. Our Christian experience of the present moment is made from these two modes of time, and this means that we Christians are in eschatological tension.[5] The decisive act of Christ's redemption already took place when we confessed our faith in Christ and were baptized; yet the final completeness and changeless happiness are still in the future dimension. The ancient Hebrews already experienced God's great hands when they were delivered from the Egyptian slavery and crossed the Red Sea in the Exodus event. Yet they were still wandering about in the wilderness hoping to see the promised land of milk and honey. We Christians are also in the wilderness of the existential, eschatological tension between the past and the future. We may call this an existential spatio-temporal situation. However, this spatio-temporal situation is transformed and sanctified into trans-spatial and trans-temporal dimensions through the eternal high priesthood of Christ and his mediation in heaven, while the Hebrew ancestors were still remaining in the mundane space and time situation, even after entering the promised land.

The above considerations are to show how important and meaningful the study of space and time language is in connection with Christian liturgical worship, especially the Eucharist which is the core of Christian faith and life, and in connection with the theology and experience of the church. The knowledge and experience of liturgical spatio-temporal language is of vital importance and effectiveness to our hermeneutic work. When a Christian teacher or preacher has an adequate knowledge of such a hermeneutic language and meaning, his faith and work will be more meaningful and effective.

NOTES

Chapter I

1. Anthony C. Thiselton, *The Two Horizons*, p. 3.
2. *Ibid.* H. Thielicke, "The Restatement of New Testament Mythology" in Kerygma and Myth 1, p. 149.
3. W. H. Halverson, *A Concise Introduction to Philosophy*, p. 5.
4. John Macquarrie, *In Search of Humanity*, p. 65.
5. *Ibid.* , p. 59.
6. Paul M. Van Buren, *The Secular Meaning of the Gospel*, p. 16.
7. H. P. Owen, *Revelation and Existence*, p. 1.
8. John Macquarrie, *The Scope of Demythologizing*, (Here after cited as Scope.), p. 33.
9. Amos N. Wilder, *Early Christian Rhetoric, the Language of the Gospel*, p. 10.
10. *Kerygma and Myth*, (ET), ed. Hans Werner Bartsch, pp. 1-2.
11. The Spatio-temporal Semantics is my own term.
12. *Kerygma and Myth, op. cit.* , p. 12.
13. *Ibid.*
14. For the new hermeneutical theories, see especially Hans-Georg Gadamer, *Truth and Method* (ET) and Paul Ricoeur, *Interpretation Theory.*
15. Sandra M. Schneiders, "The Paschal Imagination: Objectivity And Subjectivity In New Testament Interpretation" in *Theological Studies* March 1982, Vol. 43, No. 1. p. 58.
16. *Ibid.*
17. *Ibid.*
18. Wolthart Pannenberg, *Basic Questions in Theology*, Vol. 1. p. 109.
19. S. M. Sneiders, *op. cit.* , p. 62., Gadamer's *Truth and Method*, (hereafter cited as T.& M.) p. 341, Ricoeur's Interpretation Theory p. 93.

20. A. M. Johnson, Jr., *Structural Analysis and Biblical Exegesis*, p. 20.
21. *Ibid.* , p. 8.
22. *Ibid.* , p. 22
23. P. Ricoeur, *Interpretation Theory*, p. 87.
24. Norman Perrin, *Jesus and the Language of the Kingdom*, pp. 171ff.
25. Wilbur M. Urban, *Language and Reality*, p. 145.
26. P. Ricoeur, *op. cit.* , p. 63.
27. *Ibid.* , p. 10.
28. W. Urban, *op. cit.* , p. 744.
29. *Ibid.* , p. 150.
30. For Further explanation, See p.p. 105ff.
31. *Encyclopedia Britannica*, vol. 12. pp. 21-22.
32. Paul Tillich, *Theology of Culture*, p. 30.
33. *Ibid.* , p. 39.
34. See below, p.p. 60ff.
35. H. G. Gadamer, T. & M. p. 350.
36. *Ibid.* , p. 345.
37. *Ibid.* , p. 350.
38. *Ibid.* , p. 353.
39. S. M. Schneiders, *op. cit.* , p. 59.
40. *Ibid.* , p. 57.
41. Kerygma and Myth (ET) pp. 1-44.
42. K. Jaspers and R. Bultmann, *Myth And Christianity*, pp. 3-4.
43. S. M. Schneiders, *op. cit.* , p. 55.
44. T. & M. pp. 475-478.

Chapter II

1. Bultmann, *Jesus Christ and Mythology*, p. 19.
2. *Kerygma and Myth*, p. 10.
3. *Ibid.* , p. 10, n. 2.
4. *Ibid.* , pp. 11-12.
5. J. Macquarrie, *An Existentialist Theology*, p. 29ff.
6. *Jesus Christ and Mythology*, p. 68.
7. *Ibid.* , p. 68.
8. *Ibid.* , p. 20.
9. *Ibid.*

10. *Ibid.* , p. 22.
11. *Ibid.* , p. 45.
12. Macquarie, *Scope,* p. 46ff. L. Malevez, *The Christian Message and Myth,* p. 29ff.
13. *Scope,* pp. 148-149. Cf. Edwin Good, "The Meaning of Demythologization" in *The Theology of Rudolf Bultmann,* (ed.) by Charles W. Kegley, p. 24, n. 6.
14. *Jesus Christ and Mythology,* p. 53.
15. *Ibid.* , p. 49
16. *Ibid.* , p. 50
17. *Ibid.* , p. 45
18. *Scope,* p. 36.
19. *Ibid.* , p. 36ff.
20. *Ibid.* , p. 224.
21. R. W. Hepburn, "Demythologizing and the Problem of Validity" in *New Essays in Philosophical Theology* (ed.) by A. Flew & A. MacIntyre, p. 229.
22. *Scope,* p. 187.
23. *The Secular Meaning of the Gospel,* p. 58. Cf. S. Ogden, *The Reality of God,* p. 117.
24. *Kerygma and Myth,* p. 196.
25. *Scope,* p. 202.
26. *Jesus Christ and Mythology,* p. 68.
27. Wilbur M. Urban, *Language and Reality,* p. 424.
28. *Ibid.* , p. 593
29. Edwin Bevan, *Symbolism and Belief,* p. 29.
30. *Ibid.*
31. John MacMurray, *The Self as Agent,* pp. 27-28.
32. *Language and Reality,* pp. 186-187.

Chapter III

1. Giovanni Miegge, *Gospel and Myth,* p. 108.
2. R.H. Fuller, *The New Testament in Current Study,* pp. 22-23; A. Wilder, *New Testament Faith for Today,* pp. 38-71; S. Johnson, *ATR,* 36, I, (January 1954), "Bultmann and the Mythology of the New Testament", pp. 29-47.
3. Burton H. Throckmorton, Jr., *The New Testament and Mythology,* p. 94.
4. *Ibid.* , pp. 96-97.

5. For the full discussion of theory about myth, see John McKenzie's *Myth and Reality*, Chapter 9, pp. 182-186.
6. J. McKenzie, *Ibid.* , pp. 187-188.
7. Ernst Cassirer, *The Philosophy of Symbolic Forms*, Vol. 2, p. 74.
8. J. Macquarrie, *God-Talk*, pp. 173-174, 193.
9. E. Bevan, *Symbolism and Belief*, p. 11.
10. F.W. Dillistone (ed.) *Myth and Symbol,* p. 4.
11. *Ibid.* , p. 5.
12. *Ibid.* , p. 6.
13. A.C. Thiselton, *Language Liturgy and Meaning*, p. 22.
14. *Myth and Symbol*, p. 6.
15. *Thiselton, op. cit.* , p. 22.
16. Paul Tillich, *Systematic Theology*, Vol. 1, p. 239.
17. *Ibid.* , p. 240.
18. *Ibid.* , p. 241.
19. *Ibid.*
20. Urban, *Language and Reality*, p. 621.
21. Thiselton, *op. cit.* , p. 23.
22. Bevan, *Symbolism and Belief*, p. 224.
23. A. Jeffner, *The Study of Religious Language*, p. 57.
24. J. Macquarrie, *God-Talk*, p. 219.
25. Thiselton, *op. cit.* , p. 24.
26. *Ibid.*
27. Tillich, *Systematic Theology*, Vol. I, pp. 192-193.
28. *Ibid.* , p. 194.
29. *Ibid.*
30. Urban, *Language and Reality*, pp. 185-186.
31. Tillich, *Systematic Theology*, Vol. I, pp. 264-265.
32. *Ibid.* , Vol. II, p. 10.
33. *God-Talk*, p. 51.
34. *Systematic Theology*, Vol. I, p. 274.
35. *Ibid.* , p. 275.
36. *Ibid.*
37. *Ibid.* , p. 276.
38. *Ibid.*
39. *Ibid.* , p. 277.
40. *Ibid.* , p. 278, n. 9.
41. *Language Liturgy and Meaning*, p. 23, n. 4.
42. G. Miegge, *Gospel and Myth*, p. 119ff.
43. B. Throckmorton, *The New Testament and Mythology*, p. 96.

44. *Ibid.* , p. 118.
45. *Ibid.* , p. 86.

Chapter IV

1. For their discussion of hermeneutics, see Robert Funk's *Language, Hermeneutic and Word of God,* pp. 47-71.
2. L. Wittgenstein, *Philosophical Investigations,* Section 23.
3. *Ibid.* , Section 25.
4. *Ibid.* , Section 88.
5. *Language Liturgy and Meaning,* p. 5.
6. Urban, *Language and Reality,* p. 197.
7. *God-Talk,* p. 91.
8. Urban, *op. cit.* , p. 186. Urban's conception might be compared with Bultmann's *Entmythologisierung,* but in the two terms, there is big difference. Whereas the use of the former is inseparable from linguistic symbolism, the latter is exposed to criticism of *Entsymolisierung.* See J. Macquarrie, *Scope,* p. 205.
9. Urban, *op. cit.* , pp. 116-117.
10. *God-Talk,* p. 159.
11. *Scope,* pp. 193-194.
12. Urban, *op. cit.* , p. 185.
13. *Scope,* pp. 195-196.
14. Urban, *op. cit.* , p. 619.
15. *Ibid.* , pp. 622-624.
16. *God-Talk,* p. 166.
17. *Ibid.* , pp. 166-167.
18. Urban, *op. cit.* , p. 623.
19. *Ibid.*
20. T. & M. pp. 399-400.
21. *Ibid.* , p. 405.
22. Urban, *op. cit.* , p. 22
23. *Ibid.* , p. 107.
24. *Ibid.* , p. 140.
25. *Ibid.* , p. 99.
26. *Ibid.* , p. 101.
27. *Ibid.*
28. *Ibid.* , p. 239.

29.   John Searle, "Chomsky's Revolution in Linguistics" in *On Noam Chomsky: Critical Essays*, p. 9.
30.   *Ibid.* , p. 5.
31.   *Ibid.* , p. 29.
32.   *Ibid.*
33.   W. Urban, *op. cit.* , p. 151.
34.   P. Ricoeur, *op. cit.* , pp. 1ff.
35.   *Ibid.* , pp. 10-11.
36.   Urban, *op. cit.* , p. 155.
37.   *Ibid.*

Chapter V

1.   John Knox, *Myth and Truth -- An Essay on the Language of Faith* -- p. 47.
2.   For Bultmann's references to mythological language (space and time), see *Kerygma and Myth*, pp. 15-16. Throckmorton, *op. cit.* , pp. 20-22.
3.   W. Urban, *op. cit.* , p. 706.
4.   See pp. 47-48.
5.   A. Wilder, *op. cit.* , p. 33.
6.   Cf. Throckmorton, *op. cit.* , p. 89.
7.   J. Macquarrie, *God-Talk*, p. 172.
8.   W. Urban, *op. cit.* , p. 465.
9.   *Ibid.* , p. 574.
10.   For more examples of Old Testament drama; Exodus (spatial), covenant story at Sinai (height), Jacob's story (time), etc.
11.   J. Macquarrie, *God-Talk*, p. 172.
12.   *Ibid.* , p. 177.
13.   Herbert Richardson, *Theology For a New World*, p. 51.
14.   J. Macquarrie, *God-Talk*, p. 178.
15.   *Ibid.*
16.   *Ibid.* , pp. 173-174, 193.
17.   See p. 102f.
18.   W. Urban, *op. cit.* , p. 426.
19.   J. Macquarrie, *op. cit.* , p. 228.

Chapter VI

1. Cf. W. Urban, op. cit., Chapter 3, "Language as the bearer of meaning", pp. 95-133.
2. *Ibid.*, p. 117.
3. *Ibid.*, p. 119.
4. J.J. Jackson, "Deep", *IDB*, Vol. 1, pp. 813-814. T.H. Gaster, "Cosmogony", *IDB*, Vol. 1, p. 702f. (*IDB* : Interpreter's Dictionary of the Bible)
5. B.W. Anderson, "Creation", *IDB*, Vol. 1, p. 726. Cf. A Richardson, *op. cit.*, pp. 206-207. *Tiamat* is etymologically related to Hebrew, *tehom.*
6. J.J. Jackson, *op. cit.*, pp. 813-814. R.N. ワイプレ著（村上達夫）　現代の旧約聖書釈義　　　　p. 19.
7. T. H. Gaster, "Myth, Mythology" *IDB*, Vol. 3, p. 482.
8. For the primacy of space language, see Urban, *op. cit.*, pp. 185-186.
9. Cf. V.H. Kooy, "Symbolism" *IDB*, Vol. 4, pp. 472-473.
10. Bultmann, *Theology of the New Testament*, Vol. 1, pp. 164-167.
11. *Ibid.*, Vol. 2, p. 13.
12. A. Richardson's contention is that the New Testament view of the $\kappa \acute{o} \sigma \mu o \varsigma$ differs from Gnostic and Hellenistic views in that it does not conceive the material world to be evil. *An Introduction to the New Testament*, p. 207.
13. Bultmann, *op. cit.*, pp. 166-167.
14. A. Wilder, *op. cit.*, p. 33.
15. W. Urban, *op. cit.*, p. 706.
16. E. Bevan, *Symbolism and Belief*, pp. 29-30.
17. Cf. J.W. Bowman, "Eschatology of the New Testament", *IDB*, Vol. 2, p. 136.
18. Cf. Bultmann, *History and Eschatology*, p. 31.
19. H.K. McArthur, "Parousia", *IDB*, Vol. 3, pp. 658-659.
20. *Ibid.*
21. Throckmorton, *op. cit.*, p. 152. "Exorcisms in the New Testament are eschatological in character".
22. E. Cassirer, *op. cit.*, Vol. 1, pp. 215-216.

23. Cf. John Mash, "Time, Season" in *A Theological Word Book*, pp. 258-267.
24. E. Bevan, *op. cit.* , p. 83. "Eternity is not time prolonged to infinity: it is the negation of time, something without duration, without successiveness".

Chapter VII

1. Bultmann, *Kerygma Und Mythos* (1), p. 22, note 2. For its English translation, see *Kerygma and Myth*, p. 10, note 2.
2. *Ibid.* , p. 26.
3. Hans Conzelmann, tran. by G. Buswell, *The Theology of St. Luke*, New York, Harper and Brothers, 1960.
4. E. Dinkler, "Myth in the New Testament" *IDB.* , Vol. 3, pp. 487-488.
5. F.C. Grant, *An Introduction to New Testament Thought*, p. 227.
6. Jean Daniélou, S.J., *The Bible and the Liturgy*, p. 308.
7. *Ibid.* , p. 316.
8. J. Macquarrie, *God-Talk*, pp. 174, 194.
9. A. Richardson, *op. cit.* , p. 117.
10. J. Macquarrie, *op. cit.* , pp. 171-178. Of his seven characteristics, four are adopted in this thesis.
11. A. Richardson, *op. cit.* , p. 204.
12. Herbert Richardson, *op. cit.* , p. 661.
13. E. Bevan, *op. cit.* , p. 28.
14. Throckmorton, *op. cit.* , p. 118.
15. G.H.C. Macgregor, *The Interpreter's Bible* (Acts) pp. 29, 31.
16. John Marsh, *op. cit.* , pp. 258-267.
17. Alan Richardson, *op. cit.* , p. 194.
18. R. H. Fuller, *Preaching the New Lectionary*, p. 193.
19. A. Richardson *op. cit.* , p. 65.
20. Erich Fromm, *Man For Himself - An Inquiry into the Psychology of Ethics*, p. 66.
21. *Ibid.* , p. 105.
22. *Ibid.* , p. 107.
23. *Ibid.* , p. 95.

24. J. Macquarrie, *Christian Hope*, pp. 8-9.
23. *Ibid.* , p. 9.
26. See below, p. 202, 206. pp. 208ff.
27. M. Eliade, *The Sacred and the Profane: The Nature of Religion*, cf. Marion J. Hatchett, *Sanctifying Life, Time and Space*, p. 181.

Chapter VIII

1. L. Wittgenstein, *Philosophical Investigations*, Sections 19 and 23.
2. J. Macquarrie, *Paths in Spirituality*, p. 58.
3. *Ibid.* , p. 73
4. *Ibid.* , pp. 82-93
5. 中川秀恭 著 ヘブル書研究 pp. 294-295.

BIBLIOGRAPHY

Achtemeier, P. J., An Introduction to the New Hermeneutic, Philadelphia, Westminster Press, 1969.

Allegro, John M., The Sacred Mushroom And The Cross, London, Hodder & Stoughton, 1970

Alston, W.P., Philosophy of Language, Englewood, Prentice-Hall, 1964.

Altizer, Thomas, Oriental Mysticism and Biblical Eschatology, Philadelphia, Westminster Press, 1961.

Ayer, A.J., Language, Truth and Logic, London, Gollancz, 2nd edition, 1964.

Barr, James, Biblical Words for Time, London, SCM, 1962.

Barr, James, Comparative Philology and the Text of the Old Testament, London, Oxford University Press, 1968.

Barr, James, Old and New in Interpretation, London, SCM, 1966.

Barr, James, The Semantics of Biblical Language, London, Oxford University Press, 1961.

Barthel, Pierre, Interpretation du Language Mythique et Theologique Biblique, Leiden, Brill, 1963.

Bartsch, Hans Werner, (ed.), Kerygma and Myth, Vol. 1 (ET by R.H. Fuller), London, S.P.C.K., 1957.

Bartsch, Hans Werner, Kerygma and Myth, Vol. 2 (ET by R.H. Fuller), London, S.P.C.K., 1962.

Bergson, Henry, Time and Free Will, (ET), New York, Harper Touchbook, 1960.

Bevan, Edwyn, Symbolism and Belief, London, George Allen & Unwin, Ltd., 1938.

Boman, Thorlief, Hebrew Thought Compared with Greek, London, SCM, 1960.

Bonhoeffer, Dietrich, Christology, London, Collins, 1966.

Bonino, Jose Miguez, Doing Theology in a Revolutionary Situation, Philadelphia, Fortress Press, 1975.

Bouyer, Louis, Liturgical Piety, Indiana, University of Notre Dame Press, 1955.

Bouyer, Louis, A History of Christian Spirituality, Vol. 3, New York, Seabury Press, 1982.

Braaten, Carl E., and Roy A. Harrisville, (trans. and ed.) The Historical Jesus and Kerygmatic Christ, New York, Abingdon Press, 1964.

Braaten, Carl E., and Roy A. Harrisville, (trans and ed.), Kerygma and History, New York, Abingdon Press, 1964.

Bultmann, Rudolf, Essays - Philosophical and Theological, (ET), Ch. 12, 'The Problem of Hermeneutics', New York, Macmillan Company, 1955.

Bultmann, Rudolf, Form Criticism (ET), New York, Harper & Row, 1962.

Bultmann, Rudolf, History and Eschatology (ET), New York, Harper & Brothers, 1959.

Bultmann, Rudolf, Jesus and the Word (ET), New York, Charles Scribner's Sons, 1958.

Bultmann, Rudolf, Jesus Christ and Mythology, London, SCM, 1964.

Bultmann, Rudolf, Primitive Christianity in Its Contemporary Setting, New York, Meridian Books, 1956.

Bultmann, Rudolf, Theology of the New Testament (ET), 2 vols., New York, Charles Scribner's Sons, 1955.

Buren, P.M. van, The Secular Meaning of the Gospel, London, SCM, 1959.

Buttrick, G.A. (ed.), The Interpreter's Dictionary of the Bible, 4 vols., New York, Abingdon Press, 1962.

Buttrick, G.A. (ed.), The Interpreter's Bible, 12 vols. Nashville, Abingdon, 1982.

Cairns, David, A Gospel Without Myth?, London, SCM, 1960.

Carrington, Philip, The Meaning of the Revelation, London, Society for Promoting Christian Knowledge, 1931.

Cassirer, E., Language and Myth, trans. by S.K. Langer, New York, Dover Publications, 1946.

Cassirer, E., The Philosophy of Symbolic Forms, Vols. I, II, III, trans. by Ralp Manheim, New Haven, Yale University Press, Vol. I, 1953, Vol. II, 1955, Vol. III, 1957.

Chadwick, H. Early Christian Thought in the Classical Tradition, New York, Oxford University Press, 1966.

Chomsky, N., Aspect of the Theory of Syntax, Cambridge, Mass., M.I.T., 1965.

Childs, B.S., Myth and Reality in the Old Testament, "Studies in Biblical Theology", No. 27, London, SCM, 1960.

Conzelmann, H., Grundriss Der Theologie Des Neuen Testaments, Chr. Kaiser Verlag, Munchen, 1968.

Cope, Gilbert, Symbolism in the Bible and the Church, London, SCM, 1959.

Cornfeld, G., Daniel to Paul, New York, Macmillan, 1962.

Cox, David, History and Myth, London, Darton, Longman & Todd, Ltd., 1961.

Crystal, D., Linguistics, Language and Religion, New York, Hawthorn Books, 1965.

Cullmann, O., Baptism in the New Testament (ET), London, SCM, 1950.

Cullmann, O., Christ and Time (ET), Philadelphia, Westminster Press, 1950.

Cullmann, O., The Christology of the New Testament, London, SCM, 1959.

Danielou, J., The Bible and the Liturgy, Indiana, University of Notre Dame Press, 1956.

Danielou, J., Primitive Christian Symbols, trans. by Donald Attwater, Baltimore, Helicon Press, 1964.

Diamond, A.S., The History and Origin of Language, London, Methuen & co. Ltd., 1959.

Dillistone, F.W., Christianity and Symbolism, London, Collins, 1955.

Dillistone, F.W. (ed.), Myth and Symbol, London S.P.C.K., 1966.

Dinkler, E., 'Existentialist Interpretation of New Testament', Journal of Religion, Vol. XXXII, 1952, pp. 87-96.

Dix, Gregory, The Shape of the Liturgy, London, Black, 1946.

Dodd, C.H., According to the Scripture, London, James Nisber & Company, 1953.

Dodd, C.H., The Interpretation of the Fourth Gospel, London, Cambridge, 1955.

Dudley, Guilford, The Recovery of Christian Myth, Philadelphia, Westminster Press, 1967.

Ebeling, G., Introduction to a Theological Theory of Language, England, Collins, 1973.

Ebeling, G., Word and Faith, London, Eng., SCM, 1963.

Eliade, M., Images and Symbols: Studies in Religious Symbolism, trans. by Philip Mairet, London, Harvill Press, 1961.

Eliade, M., Patterns in Comparative Religion, (ET), Bloomington Indiana University Press, 1962.

Eliade, M., The Sacred and the Profane, New York, Harper & Row, 1961.

Ellwein, E., Heilsgegenwart Und Heilszukunt Im Neuen Testament, Munchen, C. Kaiser Verlag, 1964.

Encyclopaedia Britannica, Ltd., Encyclopaedia Britannica, London, Chicago, Geneva, Sydney, Toronto, William Benton, Pub. 1964, Vol. 1 'Analogy', pp. 842-843. Vol. 21, 'Space-Time', pp. 103f.

Farrer, A.M., A Rebirth of Images, London, Dacre Press, 1949.

Farrer, A.M., Finite and Infinite, London, Dacre Press, 1943.

Farrer, A.M., The Glass of Vision, London, Dacre Press, 1948.

Ferre, F., Language, Logic and God, New York, Harper & Row, 1961.

Flew, A. and A. MacIntyre, (ed.) New Essays in Philosophical Theology, London, SCM, 1955.

Frege, Gottlob, Translations from the Philosophical Writings of Gottlob Frege, Oxford, Basil Blackwell, 1970.

Fromm, Erich, Man For Himself, Fawcett World Library, 1965.

Fuchs, Ernst, Hermeneutik, R. Mulerschon Verlag, 1964.

Fuchs, Ernst, Studies of the Historical Jesus, London, SCM, 1964.

Fuller, R.H., The Foundations of New Testament Christology, London, Lutterworth Press, 1965.

Fuller, R.H., Preaching the New Lectionary, Collegeville, The Liturgical Press, 1975.

Fuller, R.H., The New Testament in Current Study, New York, Scribner, 1962.

Funk, R.W., Language, Hermeneutic, and Word of God, New York, Harper & Row, 1966.

Gadamer, Hans-Georg, Truth and Method, New York, Crossroad, 1975.

Gilkey, L., The Renewal of God-Language, New York, The Bobbs-Merrill Company, 1969.

Glasson, T.F., Greek Influence in Jewish Eschatology, London, S.P.C.K., 1961.

Gogarten, F., Demythologizing and History, London, SCM, 1955.

Halverson, W. H., A Concise Introduction to Philosophy, New York, Random House, 1967.

Harman, Gilbert, On Noam Chomsky: Critical Essays, (ed.) New York, Anchor Press, 1974.

Hastings, J. (ed.), Dictionary of the Bible. Edinburgh, T. & T. Clark, 1904, 5 Vols.

Hatchett, M.J., Sanctifying Life, Time and Space, New York, Seabury Press, 1976.

Hedley, G., The Symbol of the Faith: As Study of the Apostles' Creed, New York, The Macmillan Company, 1948.

Henderson, Ian, Myth in the New Testament, London, SCM, 1952.

Hebert, A.G., Liturgy and Society, London, Faber, 1935.

Hebert, A.G., Scripture and the Faith, New York, Morehouse Barlow, 1962.

Heidegger, M., Being and Time, (ET), Blackwell, Oxford, 1962, rpt. 1973.

Heidegger, M., Kant and the Problem of Metaphysics, (ET) Bloomington, Indiana University Press, 1959, and London 1962.

Heidegger, M., An Introduction to Metaphysics, (ET), New Haven, Yale University Press, 1959, and London, 1959.

Heidegger, M., Existence and Being, London, Vision Press, 1968.

Hirsch, E.D. Jr., Validity in Interpretation. New Haven, Conn.: Yale University Press, 1967.

Hoijer, Harry, Language in Culture, The University of Chicago Press, 1954.

Hook, S., Religious Experience and Truth, Edinburgh, Oliver and Boyd, 1962.

Hooke, S.H., The Resurrection of Christ as History and Experience, London, Darton, Longman & Todd, 1967.

Hopper, S.R. (ed.), Spiritual Problem in Contemporary Literature, New York, Harper & Brothers, 1957.

Husserl, Edmund, Logical Investigation, (ET) 2 Vols., London, Routledge & Kegan Paul, 1970.

Jackson, Samuel Macauley, (ed.), The New Schaff-Herzog Encyclopedia of Religious Knowledge, Michigan, Baker Book House, 1964, Vol. XI, 'Symbolics', 'Symbolism', pp. 199-212.

Jaspers, K. & Bultmann, R., Myth and Christianity, New York, Noonday Press, 1958.

Jeffner, A., the Study of Religious Language, London, SCM, 1972.

Jeremias, Joachim, The Parables of Jesus, (ET). London, SCM, 1963.

Jeremias, Joachim, The Central Message of the New Testament, (ET). London, SCM. 1965.

Johnson, A.M., Structural Analysis And Biblical Exegesis, Pittsburgh, The Pickwick Press, 1974.

Jones, G.V., Christology and Myth in the New Testament, London, George Allen & Unwin Ltd., 1956.

Jung, C.G., Psychology and Religion, New Haven, Yale University Press, 1938.

Kaesmann, E., Exegetische Versuche Und Besinnungen, Gottingen, Vandenhoeck & Ruprecht, 1960.

Kaesmann, E., Das Wandernde Gottesvolk, Gottingen, Vandenhoek & Ruprecht, 1935.

Kegley, Charles, (ed.), The Theology of Rudolf Bultmann, London, SCM, 1966.

Kepler, T.S., Dreams of the Future, London, Lutterworth Press, 1963.

Kepler, T.S., The Meaning and Mystery of the Resurrection, New York, Association Press, 1963.

Kittel, G., (ed.), Theologisches Worterbuch Zum Neuen Testament, Stuttgart, W. Kohlhammer, 1932.

Knox, John, Myth and Truth - An Essay on the Language of Faith, Charlottesville, The University Press of Virginia, 1964.

Kummel, W. G., Promise and Fulfillment, London, 1957.

Langer, S.K., Philosophy in a New Key, New York, The New American Library, 1956.

Lillie, William, Jesus Then and Now, Philadelphia, Westminister Press, 1965.

Lyons, J., Structural Semantics, Blackwell, Oxford, 1963.

Macquarrie, J., An Existentialist Theology, London, SCM, 1960.

Macquarrie, J., Christian Hope, New York, The Seabury, 1978.

Macquarrie, J., God-Talk, London, SCM, 1967.

Macquarrie, J., In Search of Humanity, New York, Crossroad, 1985.

Macquarrie, J., The Concept of Peace, London, SCM, 1973.

Macquarrie, J., Principles of Christian Theology, New York, Charles Scribner's Sons, 1966.

Macquarrie, J., The Scope and Limit of Demythologizing, London, SCM, 1966.

Macquarrie, J., Paths in Spirituality, London, SCM, 1972.

Malevez, L., The Christian Message and Myth, London, SCM, 1958.

Marsh, John, The Fullness of Time, London, Nisbet, 1952.

Mashall, I.H., (ed.) New Testament Interpretation. Paternoster, Exeter, 1976.

Marty, Martin E. and Dean G. Peerman, (ed.), New Theology No. 4, New York, The Macmillan Company, 1967.

Marxsen, Willi, Anfangsprobleme Der Christologie, Gutersloh, Gerd Mohn, 1960.

Marxsen, Willi, Die Bedeutung Der Auferstehungsbotscharf Fur Den Glauben An Jesu-Christus, Gutersloh, Gerd Mohn, 1966.

Mascal, E.L., Existence and Analogy, London, longmans, 1949.

Mascal, E.L., Words and Images, London, Longmans, 1957.

McKenzie, J.L., Myths and Realities, New York, The Bruce Publishing Company, 1966.

McKenzie, J.L., Dictionary of the Bible, New York, The Bruce Publishing Company, 1965.

Meland, B., Fallible Forms and Symbols, Philadelphia, fortress, 1976.

Meland, B., The Reality of Faith, New York, Oxford University Press, 1962.

Meland, B., Faith and Culture, New York, Oxford, University Press, 1981.

Miegge, G., Gospel and Myth, Richmond, Virginia, John Knox Press, 1960.

Miegge, G., (ET), Christian Affirmations in a Secular Age, New York, Oxford University Press, 1958.

Minear, P.S., Christian Hope and the Second Coming, Philadelphia, Westminister Press, 1954.

Minear, P.S., Images of the Church in the New Testament, Philadelphia, Westminister Press, 1960.

Moltmann, J., Theology of Hope, London, SCM, 1967.

Moltmann, J., (ET) The Experiment Hope, Philadelphia, fortress Press, 1975.

Morris, C., Signs, Language and Behaviour, New York, George Braziller, Inc., 1946.

Mowinckel, S., The Psalms in Israel's Worship, Vols. 1, 2, Oxford, Basil Blackwill, 1962.

Mueller, J.J., Faith and Appreciative Awareness, Washington, D.C., University Press of America, 1981.

Ogden, S.M., Christ Without Myth, New York, Harper & Brothers, 1961.

Otto, Rudolf, The Idea of the Holy, London, oxford University Press, 1923.

Owen, H.P., Revelation and Existence, University of Wales Press, 1957.

Palmer, Richard E. Hermeneutics: Interpretation Theory in Shleiermacher, Dilthey, Heidegger, and Gadamer, Evanston, Ill: North Western University Press, 1969.

Pannenberg, Wolfhart, Basic Questions in Theology. (ET) 3 vols., London, SCM, 1970.

Perrin, Norman, Jesus and the Language of the Kingdom: Symbol and Metaphor in New Testament Interpretation, Philadelphia, Fortress,1976.

Pittenger, N., (ed.) Christ for Us Today, London SCM, 1968.

Plummer, A., Gospel According to St. Luke (ICC) Edinburgh, T. & T. Clark, 1908.

Poulet, George, Studies In Human Time (ET), New York. Harper Touchbook 1959.

Rahner, H., Greek Myth and Christian Mystery, London, Burn & Oates, 1963.

Rahner, Karl, Encyclopedia of Theology, (ed) New York, Seabury Press, 1975.

Ramsey, A.M., The Gospel and the Catholic Church, London, Longmans, 1936.

Ramsey, Ian, T., Religious Language, London, SCM, 1957.

Revesz, G., The origins and Prehistory of Language, (ET), London, Longmans, Green and Co., 1956.

Richardson, A., An Introduction to the Theology of the New Testament, New York, Harper & Row, 1958.

Richardson, A., (ed.), A Theological Word Book of the Bible, London, SCM, 1950.

Richardson, A., The Miracle Stories of the Gospel, London, SCM, 1941.

Richardson, H.W., Theology for a New World, London, SCM, 1968.

Ricoeur, Paul, Interpretation Theory: Discourse and the Surplus of Meaning, Fort Worth, Texas Christian University Press, 1976.

Ricoeur, Paul, Conflict of Interpretation: Essays in Hermeneutics, Evanston, Ill, Northwestern University Press, 1976.

Ringgren, H., The Faith of the Psalmists, Philadelphia, Fortress Press, 1963.

Robinson, J. and J. Cobb (ed.), The New Hermeneutic, New York, Harper & Row, 1964.

Robinson, J.A.T., Jesus and His Coming, New York, Abingdon Press, 1957.

Robinson, J.M., A New Quest of the Historical Jesus, London, SCM, 1959.

Rowe, W.L., Religious Symbols and God, University of Chicago Press, 1968.

Russil, D.S., Between the Testaments, London, SCM, 1960.

Sanday, W., The Life of Christ in Recent Research, Oxford, 1907, 'The Symbolism of the Bible', pp. 3-34.

Saussure, Ferdinand de, Course in General Linguistics, New York, McGraw-Hill, 1966.

Sawyer, J.F., Semantics in Biblical Research, London, SCM, 1972.

Schilpp, P.A. (ed.), The Philosophy of Ernst Cassirer, New York, Tudor Publishing Company, 1958.

Segundo, J.L., The Liberation of Theology, New York, Orbis, 1979.

Selwyn, E.G., The First Epistle of St. Peter, London, Macmillan & Company, 1947.

Stachel, Gunter, Die Neue Hermeneutick, Munchen, Kosel Verlag, 1968.

Steinbeck, J., Mythus Und Wahrheit im Neuen Testament, Munchen, Ernest Reinhardt Verlag, 1954.

Stowe, E.M., Communicating Reality Through Symbols, Philadelphia, Westminister Press, 1966.

Strobel, August, Kerygma Und Apokalyptic, Gottingen. Vandenhoeck & Ruprecht, 1967.

Teilhard do Chardin, Pierre, The Future of Man (ET), London, Colins, 1964.

Terrien, S., The Psalms and Their Meaning for Today, Indianapolis, The Bobbs-Merrill Company, 1952.

Thiselton, Anthoney C., The Two Horizons, Grand Rapid, Michigan, William B. Eerdmans Publishing Co. 1980.

Throckmorton B.H., The New Testament and Mythology, Philadelphia, Westminister Press 1959.

Tillich, P., A History of Christian Thought, (recorded and edited by Peter H. John) 2nd Edition, 1956.

Tillich, P., Dynamics of Faith, New York, Harper & Row and London, Allen & Unwin, 1957.

Tillich, P., Systematic Theology, Vols, I, II, London, Nisbet & Co., 1953.

Tillich, P., The New Being, New York, Scribner, 1955, London, SCM, 1956

Tillich, P., Theology of culture, New York, Oxford University Press, 1959.

Urban, W.M., Language and Reality: The Philosophy of Language and the Principles of Symbolism, London, George Allen & Unwin Ltd., 1st Pub., 1939.

Urmson, J.O., Philosophical Analysis, London, Oxford University Press, 1967.

Watts, A.W., Myth and Ritual in Christianity, London, Thames and Hudson, 1953.

Wheelwright, P., Metaphor and Reality, Bloomington, Indiana University Press, 1962.

Whort, B.L., Language, Thought and Reality, cambridge, Mass., M.I.T. Press, 1969.

Wilder, A., The Language of the Gospel, New York, Harper & Row, 1964,

Wilder, A., Theopoetic: Theology and the Religious Imagination, Philadelphia, Fortress, 1976.

Wittgenstein, L., Philosophical Investigation, Blackwell, Oxford, 1958.

Wittgenstein, L., Tractatus Logico - Philososkicus, London, Routledge and Kegan Paul, 1922.

Wright, E.G., God Who Acts, London, SCM, 1952.

PERIODICALS, REPORTS AND OTHER PUBLICATIONS

Ayers, R. H., "Theological Discourse and the Problem of Meaning" in Canadian Journal of Theology (Vol. XV, No. 2, April, 1969), pp. 112-121.

Bauckham, Richard, "Synoptic Parousia Parables and The Apocalypse" in New Testament Studies, Vol. 23, Jan. 1977.

Bowker, John, "Religious Studies and the Languages of Religions" in Religious Studies, Vol. 17, No. 4, Dec. 1981.

Cairns, David, "A Reappraisal of Bultmann's Theology" in Religious Studies, Vol. 17, No. 4, Dec. 1981.

Clarke, W.N., "The Natural Roots of Religious Experience" in Religious Studies, Vol. 17, No. 4, Dec. 1981.

Morreall, John, "Can Theological Language have Hidden Meaning?" in Religious Studies, Vol. 19, No. 1, March 1983.

Moule, C.F.D., "The Influence of Circumstances on the Use of Eschatological Terms" in The Journal of Theological Studies, Vol. XV, April, 1964.

Mueller, J.J., "Appreciative Awareness: The Feeling-Dimension in Religious Experience" in Theological Studies, Vol. 45, No. 1, March 1984.

O'Neill, J.D., "Bultmann and Hegel" in The Journal of Theological Studies, Vol. XXI, Part 2, Oct. 1970.

Pittenger, W.N., "Religious Language: Some Proposals" in Anglican Theological Review (reprinted from the July Number 1957), pp. 1-6.

Robinson, J.M., (ed.), "The Bultmann School of Biblical Interpretation, New Direction?", Journal for Theology and the Church, Vol. 1, New York, Harper & Row, 1965.

Schneiders, Sandra M., "The Pascal Imagination: Objectivity and Subjectivity in New Testament Interpretation" in Theological Studies, Vol. 43, No. 1, March 1982.

Shihor, Rachel, "The Intelligibility of Religious Language: Two Standpoints" in Religious Studies, Vol. 19, No. 2, June 1983.

Simpson, C.A., "An Inquiry Into the Biblical Theology of History" in The Journal of Theological Studies, Vol. XII, Pt. 1, April 1961.

Thiselton, A.C., Language Liturgy and Meaning, Grove Liturgical Study No. 2, Bramcote Notts, 1975.

Whittaker, John H., "Literal and Figurative Language of God" in Religious Studies, Vol. 17, No. 1, March 1981.

Subject Index

Action, 145-6, 150-1. See also
   dynamism of language,
   verb.
Action language, 157
Actuant, 17
Adjective, adjectival entity, 19,
   79-80
Allegory, 71
A-logical intuitionism, 19. See
   also Bergson.
Alpha (and *Omega*), 22, 112, 126,
   159
Analogy, and analogical, 33, 40-1,
   49, 52, 70-2, 99, 106
Anthropology, anthropological,
   40-1, 152-3,
   Anthropocentric, 13
Anxiety, 32, 50, 52-3, 158
Apocalyptic writings, 103
Apologist, 7
Archetype, 47
Aristotelian epistemology, 29
Ascension, ascending, 10-1, 88,
   113-6, 118-23, 125-8, 131-4,
   140-2, 157-8
Ascension story, 81, 83, 95, 97, 102,
   114-20, 137, 140, 151, 163,
   166-7
Atonement, 156-9
Authentic existence, 32. See also
   Heidegger.
Authority, 125
Autonomy, See semantic
   autonomy.

Baptism, 140
Beauty, 28, 155
Being, 47, 49, 65-6
Being and language, 65, Being-
   lanugage, 51, Ground of, 47,
   51 mysterious Being, 106
Behavioral language, 150
Bible, Scripture, 3, 23, 27-8, 34-6,
   48, 54-5, 81, 147-8, 153
Biblical language, 55, 61, 74,
   141-2.   New Testament
   Language, 89

Catholic Modernism,   See
   Modernism.
Christology, 18, 21, 62, 81-2, 88, 97,
   107, 112, 115, 117-8, 130, 142
Chronos, 88, 112, 124
Church, 7, 118, 145-9, 152-3, 156
Cognition, cognitive language, 5,
   49, 149
Communication, 7, 39, 40, 62, 71,
   73, 75-7, 81-2, 101-2, 129, 131,
   148-9, 151, 153
Community, communal factor,
   94-5, 102, 119, 136, 141, 148
Conceptualism, 149
Connotation, 71-2, 96, 110, 135
Content, ontological, 65. See also
   form and content.
Cosmology, 9, 17, 23, 25, 42, 65-6,
   81, 88, 111, 113-5, 126, 133
Creation, 90, 109, 114, 125, 133,
   Doctrine of. 156

185

Name Index

Biblical References

Genesis
1:2	101
1:14-18	79
5:24	119
7:11	101
9:12-15	101

Exodus
40:34f	131

Deuteronomy
10:14	97

Judges
10:18	104

1 Kings
8:27	57,97-8

Nehemiah
2:6	106

Job
11:21	98
41:1	101

Psalms
24:2	101
72:5,7,17	98
85:10-3	22
89:9f	101
102:25-7	98
104:5	101
110:1	158
113:4f	22
115:	154
148:4	97,101

Isaiah
32:2	22
40:12	98
51:6	98
66:1	98

Jeremiah
31:35	98

II Maccabees
8:12	106

III Maccabees
3:17	106

Ecclesiasticus
44:16	119

Jubilees
4:23	119

1 Enoch
39:3f	119

Matthew
11:2-6	108
12:28	108
17:5	131
23:39	124
24:3	109
24:	138
25:1-13	107
25:14-30	107
28:8-10	127
28:16-20	127
28:17	140
28:29	138

Mark
1:10	106
1:15	106
1:22	147
2:27	147
3:27	106
9:7	131
9:2-9	91,119
10:5-9	147
13:	108
14:62	119
16:9-20	116
16:16	127

Luke
1:35	168
7:18-23	106
9:34	119,131
11:20	108
16:19-31	91
19:18	107
24:49,53	117
24:50-3	128;140
29:12-27	109

John
1:14	82,130